Hiking Trails
of
Southwestern
Colorado

HIKING TRAILS
of Southwestern
C·O·L·O·R·A·D·O

THIRD EDITION

Paul Pixler

PRUETT PUBLISHING COMPANY
BOULDER, COLORADO

First edition published 1981. Third edition 2000.
Printed in the United States of America

09 08 07 06 05 04 03 02 01 00   5 4 3 2 1

Library of Congress Cataloging-in-Publication Data

Pixler, Paul, 1920–
    Hiking trails in southwestern Colorado / Paul Pixler.—3rd ed.
        p.   cm.
    Includes index.
    ISBN 0-87108-911-4
    1. Hiking—Colorado—San Juan National Forest—Guidebooks.
    2. Hiking—Colorado—Uncompahgre National Forest—Guidebooks.
    3. San Juan National Forest (Colo.)—Guidebooks. 4. Uncompahgre
National Forest (Colo.)—Guidebooks. 5. Colorado Trail (Colo.)—
Guidebooks. I. Title.

GV199.42.C62 S265 2000
917.88'25—dc21   00-036604

To my wife, Bettie, and the hikers who have accompanied me on many of these trails: Adeline Becay, John Fleming, Charlotte Hammond, Audine Hayden, Anne Pixler, Glenn Phillips, Ed and Winnie Sinden, Diane Skinner, and Marianna Stanley.

Contents

Hikes out of Silverton

The Area Fourteeners

The Colorado Trail

Preface to Third Edition

Why a third edition? Quite a bit of new material is presented in this edition because many new trails have become available. There are a couple of excellent new maps. Several trails have important changes, either internally or at their accesses and some older trails have been linked together. Trail building has become a high priority in Durango. Mountain bikes were being used at the time of the last edition, but this sport has grown immensely since that time. Many mountain bikers think of Durango as the Mountain Bike capital of the world. Indeed, Durango has produced many individuals of both sexes who have been highly ranked in world-championship races. On some trails, bikers are now the dominant users. This, along with lots of enthusiastic hikers and horseback riders, has pushed interest in trail building and usage greatly.

Bikers can move over the trails much faster than hikers, which means that they are always hungry for more and longer, more challenging trails.

Trails 2000 has been organized to promote public interest in trails and trail building. Bill Manning, the director of this group, has promoted this interest and has enlisted volunteers to build much new trail and help with upkeep. I want to express my thanks to him and to his group. I asked him for a description of the group and its work and include it here:

"Trails 2000 is a trails advocacy group in Southwest Colorado. They are headquartered in Durango and coordinate with all land management agencies, the business community, and the public. The purpose is to fix and link trails, sign and map systems, and educate users. Founded in 1990, its volunteers accomplish most of the work, with organization provided by the group director, Bill Manning.

"Trails 2000 saved an existing network of trails from development on the west side of town. They facilitated a land purchase for the public and raised money to establish the Durango Mountain Park, currently 171 acres and growing. The group fostered the Telegraph Trail System on the east side of town. They worked with a generous private landowner and brokered another deal to bring 10 miles of trail into public ownership. Trails gifted to the public link with others into a system of over 20 miles of pathways right next to Durango. Other accomplishments include helping the Forest Service establish the Dry Fork Loop and Log Chutes Trails. Energetic volunteers have also contributed thousands of hours of trail maintenance every year to keep trails in good shape."

Bill refers to signs and maps. Two very good new maps have come out of this effort, and I am using them in this edition, with appreciation for and permission of their producers:

1. Durango Area Recreation Map, cooperatively sponsored by City of Durango Parks and Recreation, La Plata County, Colorado Division of Wildlife, San Juan National Forest and San Juan Field Office-BLM, San Juan Mountain Association, D-GO Bike Maps.

2. Durango Colorado, Telegraph Trail Network Map—D-GO Bike Maps, P.O. Box 97, Durango, CO 81302, and Goff Engineering, 126 Rock Point Dr., Durango, CO 81301.

Introduction

Why hike in southwestern Colorado? Because hiking is great fun and a healthy activity; because there is hardly a better place on earth to hike than southwestern Colorado. It offers a variety of terrain and altitude on large amounts of public land, an excellent and varied climate, and exceptionally beautiful scenery.

The lower altitudes can be hiked typically from April through November, with some hiking, especially when aided by snowshoes, available the rest of the year. Altitudes up to 10,000 feet can be hiked without special snow equipment typically from late May to early November if you do not go into heavily shaded areas. Above 10,000 feet, the season is shorter, typically late June until early fall snows, which usually are not permanent until after the middle of October or even later, depending on the particular year and the altitude.

The area offers vast hiking opportunities; this guidebook covers much of the best of it, but it cannot cover all of it. The hikes selected for inclusion here use Durango and Silverton as the starting points for directions. All of the hikes are near these two towns and include several spots between the two.

The hikes are planned for half-day and full-day trips. This is not a backpacker's book, although some of the trails are useful for that if anyone wants to take them at a very leisurely pace. A few of the hikes are best handled by driving in the day before the hike and car-camping. But for all of the trips in this book, only a day pack is needed. With its lighter weight, it is a more pleasant burden.

The hikes described range from easy to difficult, from short to long, from relatively level to some long climbs. All types of hikers should be able to find something to suit their own tastes. None of the climbs require any technical gear or skills. Some places pose a degree of danger, but these only require carefulness. Cliff edges, for example, should always be approached cautiously, but they frequently furnish breathtaking views and are safe to anyone exercising due care. Of course, you should make sure that the cliff edge is not cracking away before trusting it.

Most of the hikes are exclusively on public land. A few national forest trails cross private land, and the forest service has made proper arrangements with owners. Occasionally public and private lands are so intermixed that boundaries cannot be identified. This is particularly true of small patented mining claims in mineralized areas as, e.g., in some spots of La Plata Canyon. There are also a few places in or near Durango where private property may be crossed. Where private property is identifiable, due care for private rights should be exercised as appropriate anywhere, whether in the mountains or in town.

The Headings

At the beginning of most of the hike descriptions, I have listed information about each trail to aid the hiker judge key issues. For a few of the hikes, especially the city hikes, I included this information in the running text instead of providing a list. Some explanation of the list is due.

After the *name* of the hike comes the *distance*. This is identified as one way or round trip. It is difficult to be accurate on distances, but they should give some help in estimating time involved; however, this will vary from person to person, from steep uphill to flat or downhill, and from smooth to rough. The average hiker takes about twice as long to go up steep terrain as to descend. The higher the altitude, the greater will be the differential.

Elevations are given for the starting and highest points; total *elevation gain* is also listed. This gives some clue to difficulty and steepness when compared to distance. Usually, altitude gain is the simple difference between starting point and high point, but in some cases, where an intervening loss must be regained, total gain will be more. The level of difficulty depends on altitude to be climbed and on steepness and roughness. The rating system takes all of these into consideration. Also, a 1,000-foot climb that begins at 6,000 feet is much easier than a 1,000-foot climb that starts at 13,000 feet.

Higher altitudes are in themselves a hazard to some people. To those who live in Durango or Silverton or similar elevations and who are in good health and are used to some exercise, any altitude in Colorado should pose no special problem. People coming into this area from low altitudes may experience some difficulty. Some visitors are breathless even in town.

Altitude affects you in several ways, most of which are dependent on the lowered atmospheric pressure and a resulting lower oxygen content per breath. If you find yourself panting at or below 10,000 feet with very little effort expended, you are not ready for any long hikes described here. Also, people with a history of heart problems or high blood pressure should probably consider only the easier and lower hikes.

Acclimatization to high altitude seems to be basically an increase in red blood cell count, which makes for a more efficient use of the available oxygen in the thinner air. People from lower altitudes who have done some sustained (aerobic) exercise may have a higher red blood cell count and may not be as likely to have altitude problems in Colorado; others may help the situation by staying a couple of days or more at altitudes of 5,000 to 8,000 feet before climbing above 11,000 feet.

Some people even in apparent good health may have some problems. Besides shortness of breath, headaches can come on. My wife, who has lived at 6,500 feet a number of years, still can tell when we reach 10,000 feet in a car by the onset of a headache. Some may experience lightheadedness or an upset digestive system. If any of these symptoms become severe, it is a good idea to get down to a lower altitude quickly to recover from "altitude sickness." Often these symptoms will subside with a good rest and a slower pace so that the hike can be continued satisfactorily. The percentage of people who have severe problems is small, so this word of caution should not deter most people in good health from taking any of these hikes. For most, high-altitude hiking can be an exhilarating experience, especially when they top their first peak and look down with awe on the other side. It is a moment of achievement and beauty that puts a new dimension into living!

Each of the hikes is rated for level of difficulty. The ratings used are easy, moderate, difficult, and hard. Any usage of terms like these is relative to the condition and experience of each hiker, so much so that some people might regard any of these hikes easy, while someone else might regard most of them hard.

I am giving the ratings based on persons in reasonably good health and with at least a minimum level of experience with hikes of a few miles length. The ratings should fit a wide range of age groups, say ten years to seventy years or more of both sexes. Whether you agree with any ratings after trying some of these hikes will depend mostly on your physical condition. Seasoned

The Animas Canyon and the Grenadier Range from the Molas Trail.

mountain hikers are likely to think of these grades a notch or two too easy. So adjust them up or down to fit your own experience. A couple of hikes on these routes should set your proper inter-pretation of them.

Several factors are included in arriving at the ratings; these are length of the hike, altitude gain, difficulty in following the route, and difficulty in getting over the route. Of these, two are most important. First is altitude gain. Practically all of these hikes include some climbing. This makes the hike much more interesting, especially if a summit with good views is attained and if the trail takes you through changing climatic zones. Altitude gain can bring more difficulty than just increased effort, however. It can bring "altitude sickness," which will require slowing down a bit.

Mostly, climbing should be fun and a way to get good exer-cise; the fun comes through interesting observations (of vegeta-tion, animals, rocks, waterfalls, babbling brooks, and mountains), a sense of accomplishment, and companionship. But those who are in good physical condition are likely to enjoy it more than others.

The most important problem in the ratings has to do with the actual surface to be traversed. There is a great deal of dif-ference between a smooth trail and a rocky one. None of the hikes described here are technical climbs involving ropes or other special equipment, but some involve talus and some rock scrambling.

Talus, or loose rock that varies roughly from eight inches to two feet in size, is typical at altitudes above timberline and often slightly below it. Talus areas may vary from being nearly flat to being so steep that they are ready to slide with any loosening. The slide point is called the angle of repose. When the talus is this steep, great care is necessary to avoid starting a slide or even the fall of a single rock. This can endanger yourself, but it is especially hazardous for any companions below you.

The most common problem with talus is not from falling rocks but just that it is more difficult to walk on. With some expe-rience, you can walk on it almost as fast as on smooth ground; it takes concentration on each step to see that the rock about to be stepped on is firmly placed. Without this, you are likely to turn an ankle or jab a shin or ankle with a sharp-edged rock.

Rock scrambling means using the hands as well as the feet to climb over rocks. Many climbs have some of this, especially near the top. It can be fun and offer variety to a hike. It can get you over near-vertical obstacles and on to higher glory.

Talus and rock scrambling problems, unless they are minor, quickly increase the level of difficulty given in the ratings.

Time allowed is estimated for an average hiker, but, of course, there is no average hiker; so the times must be treated as guidelines, not fixed truths. Some will hike faster and some slower than that given, even though a range is estimated. The times given do not allow for time used in driving to or from trailheads. This must be estimated extra. Also, times given are for actual hiking and short breath-catching stops. If you want to take long stops for pictures, lunch, a nap on a sunny hillside, or just to drink in the beauty or to talk with a companion, these should be added to the estimates.

A word about rest stops is appropriate. At higher altitudes in steep areas, almost everyone has to rest occasionally. When you are working hard, short rests of thirty seconds to a minute and a half are best. These can be frequent if necessary. Long rests of five to twenty minutes can be devastating. In the first place, they increase the total hiking time an amazing amount, but more importantly, they make you lose your "second wind." This makes it difficult to get going again and to get up to the same pace that you were maintaining earlier with relative ease. It slows down the whole cardiovascular system and slows the efficiency that you have previously attained in your climbing muscles. You have to get your second wind all over again.

Maps can be a big help. People who are used to hiking in the eastern United States, such as along the Appalachian Trail, may not need maps there due to the heavy traffic and the well-defined trails marked with frequent cairns. Hiking in Colorado, where altitudes are higher, where terrain and climate change more, and where the whole area is so much more vast, is a much different experience.

The maps given in this book are for describing the hike, but on longer hikes, other maps are useful for showing more of the surrounding territory. Two kinds of maps are typically listed in the headings. The national forest maps show roughly where the

Looking up from the Cascade Trail through timber to Engineer Mountain.

trails go. They are limited, however, due to their small scale and their lack of altitude gradations.

The U.S. Geological Survey maps give much more detail. The 7.5-minute series of quad maps show topographical gradations of forty feet from one line to the next, with 200-foot lines heavier to delineate the larger gradations. Even these maps cannot show small cliffs that can cause significant detours from straight-line hiking. While many of the hikes are over established trails, some are not, and some of the trails have breaks in them due to inadequate maintenance; hiking at this point is "bushwhacking," i.e., finding your own way. This may literally be through the bushes, or it may be over rocks or through trees. This can add its own challenge. The hike descriptions attempt to lead you through these areas without difficulty.

National forest maps can be obtained through forest headquarters offices and ranger stations. Occasionally, you can find them in sporting goods stores. The topo maps are carried by several sporting goods stores, especially those that carry hiking and climbing gear. Sometimes they can be found in magazine stores and in libraries.

The Weather

Hikers in higher altitudes in the Rockies must always be aware of the weather. It can change from beautiful to dangerous very quickly. This is especially true from June to early September, when afternoon thunderstorms are frequent. During this period, it is better to plan to reach the highest altitude in your hike by noon if possible. These storms can be severe, even though short-lived. They can bring wind, cold, rain, and small hail, depending on the particular storm. The greatest hazard, however, is lightning. It is high-voltage static electricity and can kill or maim in a split second. High points where the charged cloud is closest are the strike points. This makes high or isolated peaks especially vulnerable. But tall trees below the peak are also frequent targets.

Any dark cloud nearby in the summer should be suspect, even if it is small. There are additional signs of an imminent lightning flash. If you are on or near a high point above surrounding territory and you hear a buzzing in the rocks, or if the hair on your arms or legs or neck, and even on your head, begins to try to stand up, you're in prime territory; get down to lower levels as fast as possible. Also, if you seek shelter from rain under a tree, make it a tree lower than others nearby.

Lightning is the worst danger from storms, but not the only one. Rocks that call for scrambling can be very slick when they get wet. Lichens on them increase this problem. When I climbed El Diente, it began drizzling just after our party started down from the top; the rocks are near-vertical and are very irregular in this area. I slipped on one that would have held easily when dry. Though I fell only three feet, that led to an edge where there was another drop followed by another and another. Fortunately, two companions were at the edge of the first one and stopped me before I could go to the next drop. Though embarrassing, it served as a reminder to me to become more cautious, but it could have been disastrous.

In the high country, it can snow any month of the year, although significant amounts are rare in the summer. Only a light coating, however, slickens up the footholds and handholds.

Another danger from rainstorms is hypothermia. This is a condition in which the core body temperature begins to drop below normal. Cold fingers and toes are uncomfortable, but a cold body core is highly dangerous. Soaked clothes and some wind can bring this on quickly at high altitudes, even in July. When you begin to shiver violently, hypothermia is starting. Companions must come to the rescue and furnish heat immediately, because the victim soon becomes disoriented and does not recognize the danger. Fires are usually out of the question because of the rain. Extra clothing will help if the situation is not too bad; also, a faster pace can help when it can be done. However, in more severe cases, skin-to-skin body heat transfer is likely to be the only answer.

Emergencies

It is best when hiking in hazardous backcountry to go in parties of not less than three. If one falls and is hurt to the point of not being able to go on, another can stay with that person while the third goes for help. The one who stays should administer first aid and keep the injured person as warm and comfortable as possible. This will call for a fire if it becomes cold or dark. The

Rock scrambling.

patient should also be given plenty of fluids, for dehydration takes place rapidly at high altitudes. Dehydration of an injured person adds to the danger as well as to the discomfort.

One of the most frequent hazards is the possibility of getting lost. While I have written this guide with a great deal of care to prevent this from happening, there is no guarantee against it. A slightly different interpretation of the text than intended can sometimes cause trouble. Also, it is possible that the text has errors, although I have tried hard to prevent this.

The best approach is not to get lost. Several things help. Keep the hiking group fairly close together. Each person should take note of prominent features in the area as guideposts, just in case. Also, a compass is a good idea; learn how to read and use it. It can be used in connection with the trail map.

Suppose you do get lost? Think through where you were just before getting lost, and take your bearings from this. Usually, the trail map should show you enough to keep drainages sorted out to the point where you can get back to the one you came up. Study over any prominent peaks, trees, or rocks that you remember seeing before, and reorient from them. Check your compass. Check the sky for direction. The sun and the moon are great

Snowshoeing.

guides when available. On a starry night with no moon, the Big
Dipper is your clue. The North Star is straight out from the lip of
the Dipper. It is a faint star; if you can't find it, the lip star of the
Dipper itself will approximate north, but it varies its position during the night. The North Star does not.

Any drainage will always eventually lead to civilization, so
you can always follow down the nearest one if all else fails. This,
however, has its drawbacks. First, it may be a long way out.
Second, drainages have their own difficulties: cliffs or waterfalls
must be skirted; cliff walls next to the stream may cause you to
walk in the water or cross the stream frequently; brush and mud
near the creek don't help. If you know that you are a considerable distance from a road, house, or camp, and if you are hope-
lessly lost, the best answer is to build a fire and make yourself as
comfortable as possible while awaiting rescue.

This treatment of emergencies and hazards may give the
impression that hiking in southwestern Colorado is highly dangerous, only to be undertaken by the experienced and the fool-
hardy; this is far from the truth. It is most likely to be highly
enjoyable, even ecstatically so, if a few proper precautions are
taken. In many years of hiking and leading hiking groups in this

area, I have only had to manage one injury of consequence. This was a broken wrist that was sustained when a fellow hiker caught his toe on a small rock. The place was nearly flat—not recognizably more dangerous than a city street curb. It was the freak combination of circumstances that could have happened anywhere. So get yourself properly prepared and head for the hills! A cellular phone in a hiking group can be a big help in an emergency.

Equipment

A part of preparation is proper equipment. There are a number of good manuals about this subject, so I will treat it quite briefly.

Any hiker's equipment starts with shoes. They should be comfortable and large enough, both in length and width, especially across the toes. The size should allow for fairly thick socks, or even two pair—one thin pair and a second thicker pair. Two pair, if one is thin and a bit slick, can reduce friction and blisters. Also, the risk of blisters, if you are prone to them, can be reduced by lubricating the skin at wear points with petroleum jelly or even margarine.

The best insurance against blisters is the right shoe. Many people think that you need a heavy and expensive hiking boot. The only real requirements are comfort and adequate protection. Lighter-weight boots with rugged treaded soles are usually adequate and will not tire you as much as heavier boots. The pair I enjoyed most and that gave me no blister problems were logger's boots. They had Vibram soles, good flexibility, good toe width, and a steel protective cover over the toes that prevents leather shrinkage as well as battering injuries. Actually, tennis or jogging shoes are fine for easy, well-worn trails where the surface is not very rocky or rough.

A day pack will be necessary for carrying food, extra clothing, a first-aid kit, water, maps, and a camera. There are many good ones. Any day pack should be waterproof to protect its contents.

Coats, jackets, sweaters, and T-shirts are all appropriate to consider for the upper body. Even in hot weather, be sure to have enough along if you are going to go up to any significant altitude. Eighty-five-degree weather can quickly change to fifty degrees or lower with a cold wind when you climb. For the upper body, layers for varying temperatures and windchill factors are best. At least one layer should be wool, for it is warm and can insulate even when wet. Down will not do any good when wet, though it is lightweight and very good when dry. There should always be a windbreaker jacket in your supply; even just a thin plastic one can be a major help. Wind seeping through sweaty or rain-soaked clothes can turn them into a deep-freeze quickly. Actually, wind is not typical in southwestern Colorado even on high peaks, but it can come up strongly without much warning. You should also have rain gear. This can be a light-weight poncho or a rain suit; even a large garbage bag will do in an emergency.

I like long pants for most hiking, though some of my friends like shorts in warm weather. In the first place, I sunburn quite easily and like to keep the least amount of skin exposed. Another important consideration against shorts is brush, and even briars, which can scratch exposed legs unmercifully.

Usually, you should also take along a warm cap capable of covering the ears, since nearly half of lost body heat can escape through the head. A pair of gloves should be included, too—they are needed at times for warmth but are often useful in rock scrambling as protection against abrasion of the skin.

There should be at least one first-aid kid in any hiking group. It should include Band-Aids, moleskin (for foot blisters), water purifier, aspirin, an Ace bandage, gauze, a sunscreen lotion, some dry matches, a compass, and a flashlight. Persons who cannot whistle naturally should carry a whistle to use as a signal if they become lost.

I like to carry a piece of one-eighth-inch nylon rope. It can be used for repairs on equipment, for shoelaces, for a makeshift arm sling, and untold other things. The sunscreen should be used regularly, for the sun burns more quickly at higher altitudes.

Finally, if you are a photographer, by all means have your camera along and handy. A pair of lightweight binoculars is often useful, too.

On trips of any significant length, be sure to take a canteen of water and usually some food. If you are an angler, you will want to carry fishing gear on the appropriate trips.

Trail Users

There are three primary recreational groups that use the trails in this book: hikers, horseback riders, and mountain bikers. There are also some people who occasionally use machines such as trail motorcycles, all-terrain vehicles (ATVs), and snow-mobiles. Traffic can therefore get a bit congested at times. All users have the right to enjoy the trails, but there is a rule about the right-of-way.

Horses are easily spooked in tight, steep places. Safety demands that they have first right-of-way priority. All others must stand aside and let them pass. Hikers are next, followed by bikers, and then the machines. In tight situations uphill travelers always have priority over downhill travelers. (The immediate tight situation may allow for some variation of these rules.)

The main overall rule is courtesy and goodwill. I have found most people on trails to be courteous; in fact, there is often a brief stop to socialize a bit and to exchange good wishes.

Bon voyage!

Hikes in and near Durango

City Trails

One might justly say that the city of Durango has become conscientious, even enthusiastic, about trails. The City Parks and Recreation Department, the county, the Colorado Division of Wildlife, the San Juan National Forest and Bureau of Land Management offices, the San Juan Mountain Association, D-GO Maps, and Trails 2000 have published a map and folder of city and nearby area trails. This map is used with their permission. There are eight trails; six of these are covered here—numbers 2 through 6. Numbers 1 and 8 are enough out of town to deserve separate sections following this one.

Centennial Nature Trail (number 2) is used by many Fort Lewis College students because it connects the lower town areas with the college campus and with **the Rim Trail (number 3).** It can be found near the junction of 6th Avenue and East 10th Street. Through a series of switchbacks, the trail moves up some 300 feet to the campus mesa, coming out on the west side of the campus just south of the lovely little chapel on the rim. A campus road called Rim Drive goes both north and south from this point. For hikers, there is also a rim trail away from the road at the edge of the rim and, in places, just beneath it. Combining this trail with campus roads from the southeast to the northeast sides of the campus makes an easy loop hike of about a mile and a half. The west and northwest parts afford nice views over the town and across the valley to the La Plata Mountains.

Chapman Hill–Lions Den Trails (number 4) can be reached by going north on the Rim Trail a little more than a quarter of a mile. At this point, you can descend Chapman Hill (the city ski area) and go down to Florida Road near the Animas River, where parking is available. Or, instead of descending, you can proceed east and north to the Lions Den, across the road from the golf course near the clubhouse. The "den" is a shelter house built during the Depression from big pieces of sandstone and has

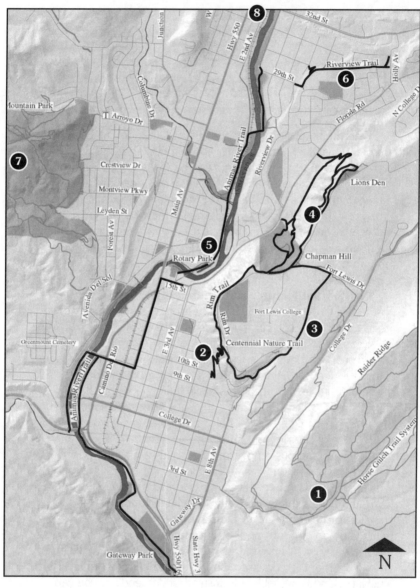

City Trails

been refurbished and roofed by the Durango Lions Club in recent years. It affords a beautiful view up the Animas Valley and beyond to some of the high San Juan peaks. The Rim Trail continues east just below this structure, but it also provides another good descent to Florida Road farther to the north than Chapman Hill. There are good switchbacks to lessen the steepness of the hillside.

Animas River Trail (number 5) is a paved route that follows the river closely almost all the way from the north end of town to the south end, but there are some gaps. Currently, it does not reach all the way to the north end. These omissions will hopefully be filled in eventually. (Trail building in Durango is a dynamic, ongoing project.) The trail is approximately four and a half miles long. It starts on the north end with the Opie Reams Trail on the east side of the river in Memorial Park, at the intersection of 29th Street and East 3rd Avenue. Good parking and restrooms are available at the trailhead. In less than a mile, the trail crosses the river over a good footbridge. It can be reached at this point either from the east via a side trail at the south end of Rio Vista Circle, or on the west, behind the high school. It continues south along the river around the end of the high school grounds, crosses a bridge over Junction Creek, and goes in back of the hospital. Then it crosses another footbridge, ending near the gazebo in Rotary Park.

From this point there is a gap down to 9th Street. If you want to hike across the gap, you can go south along Main to 9th Street and then west to the Holiday Inn next to the river. The Animas River Trail picks up again and goes behind several businesses. After the Doubletree, it goes under the U.S. Highway 160 auto bridge. It proceeds south along the highway and behind Gateway Park, goes under another highway bridge, and crosses the river to the west over an old bridge that is now closed to auto traffic. It then moves along a nice riparian area without any development for a mile. The trail ends abruptly behind a warehouse just a hundred yards short of the K-Mart store, which is the beginning of the Durango Mall. This distance can be hiked easily even though the trail officially ends. There are plans to extend it down to the new Escalante Middle School. Parts of a trail already connect the school, Sawmill Road, and Colorado State Highway 3— some of it is rough dirt and some of it is paved.

The Animas River Trail is long and will likely be made longer with extensions on both ends. Many people will be interested in hiking parts of it more often than in its entirety. There are several access points to the local segments: (1) Memorial Park at 29th Street and East 3rd Avenue; (2) south at the first footbridge (the west end can be entered behind the fairgrounds via East 2nd Street or from the high school and the east end from a short trail off the south tip of Rio Vista Circle); (3) east from the south end of the high school grounds; (4) Rotary Park (or Gazebo Park) at East 2nd Avenue and 15th Street; (5) at the east end of the 9th Street bridge behind the Holiday Inn; (6) Gateway Park; and (7) Durango Mall, 800 South Camino del Rio.

Riverview Trail (number 6) is a short trail related to Riverview Elementary School, connecting it to Holly Avenue and 31st Street.

Durango Mountain Park (number 7) encompasses a series of hills and valleys in about 2,000 acres of wild land recently acquired by the city on its western boundary. The lowest point of the park is 6,400 feet at the city boundary; the highest point is the Hogsback (discussed later) at 7,484 feet, giving a net relief of 884 feet.

There is a trail network of several miles of trails, providing some good short exploratory hikes. The map shows the recognized routes, but you can try others as well, partly on and partly off trail. Some are steep and some are gentle. During my first ten years in Durango, I lived next door to this area and spent many pleasant afternoons and evenings hiking there, both in summer and winter. Winter is also good for snowshoeing and ski touring. You could get lost in the maze of trails, but not badly, because Durango is always to the east of you and is visible from various high points.

The area is composed of Mancos shale—a gray, flaky soil that is usually soft at the surface. Some places are bare, while others have piñon pines and junipers along with some large ponderosa pines.

There are several access points. A primary one is at the west end of Leyden Street in the Crestview area. A map is posted on a sign at the trailhead. Just beyond, side trails begin branching off, one immediately to the right. Straight ahead there is a new little wooden bridge over the main arroyo. Other options soon branch off to the left uphill.

There is also access off the west ends of Montview Parkway and Arroyo Drive via Hidden Valley Circle. The last of these is a bit obscure at the start. South of Leyden, you can cross the drainage ditch at the intersection of Kearney Street and Glenisle Avenue. This route goes up steeply at first. A couple of other access routes go uphill off Avenida de Sol through short residential areas.

Durango Mountain Park is very popular with mountain bikers, and hikers need to be on the lookout for sudden biker appearances around sharp corners. Bikers owe the right-of-way to hikers, but hikers must be alert to the presence of the bikers.

Hogsback

Distance: *2 miles (round trip)*
Starting elevation: *6,641 feet*
Elevation gain: *843 feet*
High point: *7,484 feet*
Rating: *Easy, except last 200 yards*
Time allowed: *1.25 hours*
Maps: *7.5′ Durango West*

This is a part of Durango Mountain Park, located on its south boundary near the west side, but it is distinct enough to deserve special attention. It is the most challenging and most rewarding hike in the park.

Use the Leyden Street access to the park. Leyden is reached from downtown by taking 22nd Street west off Main. The street angles to the top of Crestview Mesa, where it becomes Montview Parkway; follow this west to Glenisle, then south to Leyden, and west again to the end of Leyden.

Take the trailhead across the wooden bridge. You can take the first left, which goes uphill steeply, or the second left, which is less steep. Both of these trails, at top of the first pitch, join a larger, more gradual trail that goes west toward Hogsback. The trail twists and turns through some brush, eventually reaching open shale. The last two pitches are steep but can usually be done standing up—the shale has good footholds. Near the top is

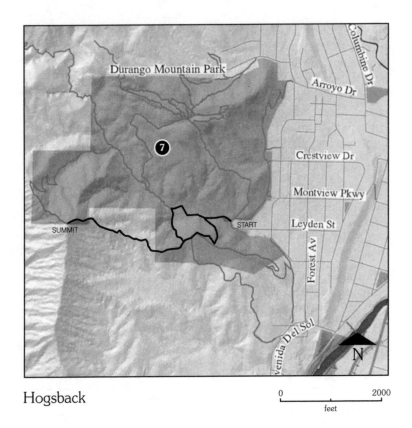

Hogsback

a very narrow spot where you must be careful not to slip, lest you take a steep, unscheduled glissade in the shale for 150 feet. The steep area is on the left part of the trail; it is a good idea to hold onto the brush on the right side. On the top there is a nice single slab of sandstone that becomes your reward for huffing and puffing. It is a good place to lie down and rest or to sit and study the city below.

Return on the same route, especially at the steep section. On the return (after the hazardous part at the top), the loose shale that was so hard to climb becomes an asset, for you can have fun shuffling down the remaining steep area.

Animas City Mountain

Distance: *6 miles (round trip)*
Starting elevation: *6,680 feet*
Elevation gain: *1,495 feet*
High point: *8,175 feet*
Rating: *Easy*
Time allowed: *3.5 to 4 hours*
Maps: *7.5' Durango East; San Juan National Forest*

This is an easy half-day hike near Durango. It is a good hike at any time of year, but it is especially appealing when the higher country is too deeply covered with snow for good hiking. This means November to June. Through the middle of the winter there is usually plenty of snow even on Animas Mountain. At that time, this becomes good territory for snowshoeing and ski touring. When the snow is deep, the elk come down to winter at this level. I have hiked this mountain many, many times; during the period from December to May, I almost always see elk and occasionally a deer. Sometimes I have seen as many as two dozen elk. They are usually about three-fourths of the way to the top. On snowy winter days they may often be seen browsing on the steep, but warm, southeast side.

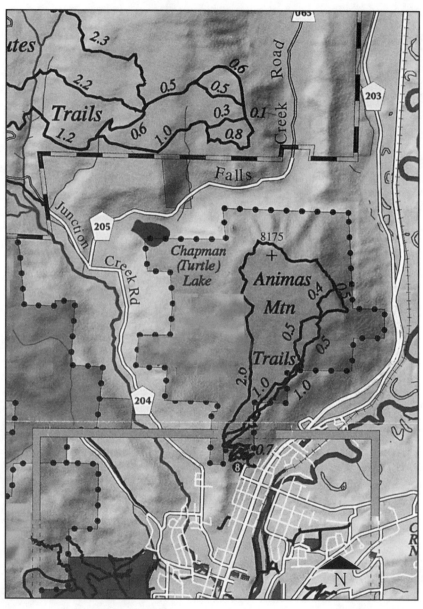

Animas City Mountain

0   1/2   1

1 mile

Overlooking Animas Valley from Animas Mountain.

To do this hike, take Thirty-Second Street west of Main in Durango to its west end on Fourth Avenue. Turn right here and follow it to the end, where there is good gravel parking for several cars. The trailhead has a sign with a map of the loop.

The east (right) side of the loop—a very popular mountain biking route—is two trails that parallel and occasionally cross each other. The purpose of the double route is to help separate bikers and hikers.

The west side of the loop is an old four-wheel-drive road that is quite rough on the lower part. You can still use this side, but the newer route is easier to climb.

After climbing a little over a mile on the east side, the trail brings you close to the rim rock where you can look down and see Durango. From this point to the northeast high point, there are several places where it is worthwhile to step off the trail and look down into the valley. At the high point there is a view of the Animas Valley and the tortuous, winding river amid pastures populated with horses and cattle. There are also some old turns of the river now bypassed and disconnected, known as "oxbows." These usually have water in them from the snowmelt. The entire scene is peaceful in contrast to so many of the rugged mountain views around Durango.

Elk on Animas Mountain in the winter.

If you take the west side of the loop, you will end up at the other high point in two and a half miles from the start. At the west side's high point, look sharply down into the Fall Creek Valley and northwest across the valley to the high La Plata Mountains. If you do the whole loop, you will also arrive at this point a half mile west of the northeast point. To complete the loop, follow the west side down to its union with the east side, which is about two miles, and then down half a mile to the starting point.

For people who like to keep their legs in good climbing condition even in the winter, I recommend climbing Animas Mountain from its steep southeast side. Snow does not usually stay long because of the angle of exposure. For this approach, leave your car in the parking lot of the North Campus Mercy Medical Center, which is located just west of Highway 550 at the north end of Durango, and start climbing from the northwest corner climbing north and west.

There is no trail, but there are plenty of open spaces in the brush and low trees. The more west you climb, the steeper it becomes; the more north you hike, the more you can ameliorate the steepness. A large elk population often winters in this steep area. The finest bull elk portrait I have ever taken was photographed in this area. About three-fourths of the way up to the rim is a nice large shelf. This is a good place to find deer and elk if you have not found them lower down. At one time I spotted a large herd here with an unusual albino elk.

Barnroof Point

Distance: *5 miles (round trip)*
Starting elevation: *6,940 feet*
Elevation gain: *1,783 feet*
High point: *8,723 feet*
Rating: *Moderate*
Time allowed: *2.5 to 3.5 hours*
Maps: *7.5'Durango West; San Juan National Forest*

Barnroof Point is on Colorado Wildlife and Bureau of Land Management property, but it shows on the forest service map. The lower part of the south and southwest sides is private property. Deer, elk, and grouse can often be seen on this mountain. Also, the top affords one of the best views of the east side of the La Platas.

Barnroof is heavily vegetated, especially with ponderosa pine and oak brush. The brush is from knee-high to ten or twelve feet. It can be a real thicket and hard to get through. Since part of this hike will require bushwhacking, you need to be aware of the oak brush problem. Staying near the east and north sides of the mountain will help you avoid most of this.

Barnroof is a low mountain east of the La Platas. It is inter-esting in that it stands as a single peak with valleys on all sides. This makes it a nice climb for presenting good views of surround-ing territory.

To start the hike, go west of Durango on Highway 160 three and one-half miles to a right turn on Lightner Creek Road. Follow it one mile north to where it turns sharply left and crosses Dry Fork. Instead of turning, go straight ahead through a gate. Park just inside. This is Colorado Division of Wildlife land. The

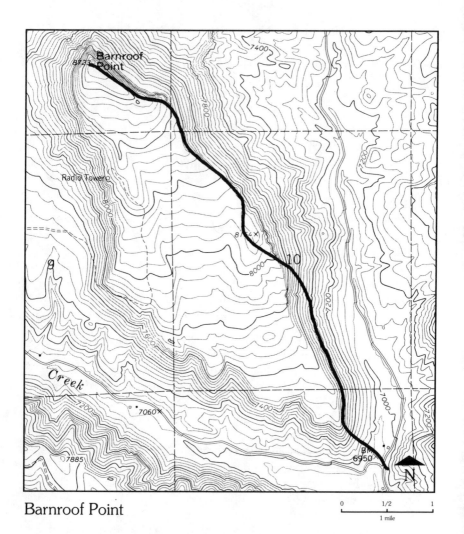

Barnroof Point

agency prohibits public access to Barnroof through the winter. It is open to hiking from April 1 to November 14.

Begin hiking west across the creek, usually a very small stream, and up the other side. In 200 yards, you should strike an old road. Take this up the east side, going north to its termination in seven-tenths of a mile. Unfortunately, it stops short of reaching the top of the steep side, so you will have to scramble up about twenty feet. Once on this rim, it will be easy going most of the way. Hike just back of the rim in a northerly direction and eventually in a northwest direction one and one-fourth miles to the top. By staying near the rim, you do not encounter much of the brush. Also, there will be many fine views of the valleys below and the peaks beyond. However, big-game animals are more likely to be back farther, even in the brush.

Just before reaching the top, you will find some interesting trenches that appear to have been caused by some ancient geological disturbances.

The view of the La Platas from the high point, the northwest corner, is great. With a deep valley between, foothills sweep upward to the rocky high peaks, forming a majestic view.

The easiest return is by the approach route, but brave souls may want to vary from that. If so, head south one-half to one mile; then veer east to strike the descent road back to the parking area. This route passes through big pines, an occasional meadow, and, unfortunately, brush thickets. These can be crossed with patience, but they are a nuisance. Perhaps you will see deer and/or an elk this way.

The last time I led a group up this mountain, we stirred up a very large bear. Fortunately, he decided to run uphill ahead of us and disappeared.

Dry Creek to Durango

Distance: *5 miles (one way)*
Starting elevation: *7,280 feet*
Elevation gain: *400 feet*
High point: *7,680 feet*
Rating: *Easy*
Time allowed: *2 to 3 hours*
Maps: *7.5' Durango West; San Juan National Forest*

This is an easy afternoon hike near Durango. Although it is on the forest service map, the route lies just outside the national forest boundary and traverses Colorado Wildlife property, a little Bureau of Land Management territory, and, for the last mile, private property. Unfortunately for hikers, the Division of Wildlife prohibits public access to this territory from November 15 to July 15. The last month of the open period is mostly hunting season, but hikers will be safe here if they wear the blaze orange required of hunters—it is remarkably visible through the woods and brush.

The private property has been developed into the Rockridge subdivision for private homes. But the developer is quite congenial to hikers; so much so that he has built a public hiking trail for the aforementioned mile, to the intersection of Borrego and Clovis drives. It follows along the north side of a nice arroyo; hikers should stay on this trail for its entire length.

This hike involves having transportation available at both ends. It is routed west to east because this involves only 400 feet of altitude gain; east to west presents 1,000 feet of gain.

As a wildlife feeding spot, this area offers good opportunities to see game animals. Deer roam here the year around; elk are present mostly during the restricted winter period. You may also see bear here from time to time, and, on occasion, wild turkey. Hunting is permitted in season. If the high country is snowed in early enough, hunting for both deer and elk can be very good here.

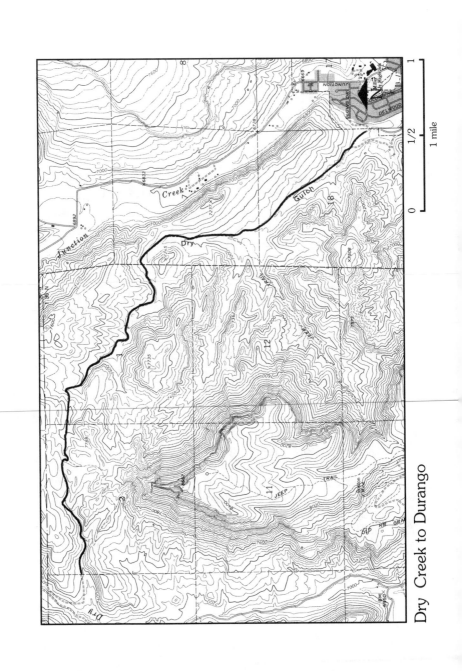

Dry Creek to Durango

To reach the hiking route, drive west of Durango three and one-half miles to a right turn on Lightner Creek Road. Follow it one mile north to where it makes a sharp turn left and crosses Dry Fork. Instead of turning, go straight ahead through a gate. This puts you into the wildlife area. Continue two miles north to where the road splits; take the right side for another quarter-mile to a cattleguard. Turn right, and go downhill in front of the guard to a parking area. The hike begins here; it ends at the intersection of Clovis and Borrego drives on the west side of Durango, where another car can be parked. To find this spot from Durango, take Twenty-Fifth Street west off north Main about a half-mile to the beginning of Clovis; turn left and follow Clovis to Borrego. The trailhead is forty yards south.

From the western parking spot, start hiking east. The first task is to cross Dry Fork; it usually is a small stream and can easily be jumped. Beyond the creek bank lies a nice meadow with a gently rising slope. Hike toward the east and a little north up this meadow; along its north side, just in the edge of the timber, you should find the remains of an old road. You follow it essentially all the way into Durango. The route rises now in less than a mile to its highest point in some big ponderosa pines. Off to the right and high above is the sharp point of the north end of the Perins Peak massif. From here on it is downhill, alternating between tall pines and open meadows. At three and one-half miles you will pass the remains of some old ranch buildings with a nice cattail pond on the right followed by another meadow. The next meadow beyond that is usually quite marshy; here it is best to cross to the south side. At four miles, you will come to private property. Take the developer's trail the last mile on to Borrego Drive.

This is a good hike, but it is not a trail recognized by the Forest Service or the Division of Wildlife for their maintenance. So in areas where the grass grows tall, it may at times be a little hard to follow. Usage helps to keep it defined.

Raider Ridge

Distance: *1 mile (round trip)*
Starting elevation: *6,600 feet*
Elevation gain: *750 feet*
High point: *7,450 feet*
Rating: *Easy*
Time allowed: *2 to 3 hours*
Maps: *7.5'Durango East; Telegraph Trail Network (available in bike stores)*

This is an easy hike out of Durango for those limited in time, but it gives a nice view down over the Fort Lewis College campus and part of Durango, and a good view of the east side of the La Platas and the south side of some of the San Juans.

"Raider Ridge" is a local name; there is no official name. This title comes from the former name of the Fort Lewis College athletic teams; they were the "Raiders." At one time, the students maintained a big "R" on the campus side of this ridge. The Raiders are now the Skyhawks, but the ridge is still called Raider.

Some of this ridge is private property; a big chunk is owned by Fort Lewis College and is open to the public. It is a steep sandstone uplift tilted ten to fifteen degrees to the southeast, known officially by geologists as a "hogback."

This has become a part of a much larger trail. It shows in the lower right-hand corner of the City Trail map as number 1. However, it is outside the city and is served by another, much better, map known as Telegraph Trail Network, used here by permission of Goff Engineering. It is listed as a D-GO Bike Map. Mountain bikers are major users, but much of the network was used by hikers before mountain bikes were invented and is still useful for hiking. Biker interests have improved the system a lot by tying together several old trails, thus extending the system.

Estimates of the total size are up to twenty miles. Hikers will not be interested in doing all of it in one hike but will be able to take a number of interesting shorter hikes.

Access is via Horse Gulch Road, which is now closed on its Durango end to motorized traffic, leaving hikers and bikers as the primary users. To take this route, follow Eighth Avenue south to 3rd Street. Go one block east on 3rd Street to its end, where it turns into Horse Gulch Road. This is a dirt road that is very rough and rocky. It goes east, later curving northeast. Park anywhere on the side after leaving the paved street. Hike a mile on Horse Gulch Road to where a side trail veers uphill to the left. Follow this trail (west) to the top of the ridge. Bikers generally turn left below the top because of the large rocks straight ahead, but hikers who go on are soon rewarded by a fine view from the top of the trail of the Fort Lewis College campus below and the La Plata Mountains rising above the valley beyond.

Hikers can now return to the bike trail or hike along the top of the ridge either south toward the beginning of Horse Gulch or north. Hiking north is interesting for up to two miles. There are several places where you can bushwhack back down to Horse Gulch Road, turning right on it to get back to your car. If you stay on top going south to where you are forced to descend, you are committed to a very steep, slippery route. It is better to drop off to the left until you strike a bike trail for an easier descent.

Sometimes Durango has a mild winter, and you can take this hike in winter as well as in other seasons. The route from Horse Gulch presents the sunny side of the ridge, where snow tends to melt fairly rapidly. Often deer and elk can be seen in this area during the winter, and deer are present year-round.

Telegraph Trail Network

This network of trails is tied in with Raider Ridge, but it all lies on the east side of Horse Gulch Road. To begin, start up Horse Gulch as explained in the Raider Ridge description; after the curve northeast, take a right turn downhill a hundred yards or more short of the left turn toward the ridge top. This goes down into a wide meadow valley and up to some higher levels, including Ewing Mesa, and several hilltops. Through the years I have hiked much of this but not all of it. There is much interesting territory to explore here. The map is your best guide. You should be able to make a series of hikes of various levels of difficulty and length. Most of the traffic is mountain bikers.

There are two other accesses. The first is at Carbon Junction, located a couple of miles south of town. Take College Drive east from Main Street to Eighth Avenue and south out of town on what becomes Colorado State Road Number 3. This parallels U.S. 160-550, which is on the west side of the river. The trail begins at Carbon Junction on the east side of the road with a big parking area, and climbs a hill through several switchbacks, working its way northeasterly and joining other parts of the Telegraph network.

The other access is more than a mile farther south around the curve to where the highway goes east, approaching the separation of the two highways at a traffic light at the beginning of Farmington Hill. A small road goes uphill on the north side a hundred yards or more west of the traffic light, rising up into a wild, wooded area that becomes Grandview Ridge Trail and that eventually joins the rest of the network.

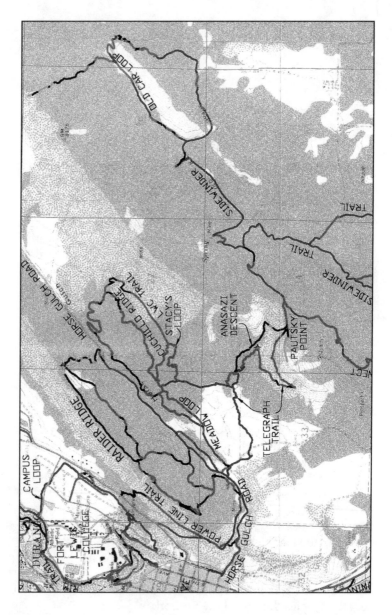

Raider Ridge and Telegraph Trail Network. This map shows Raider Ridge near the top of the trails to the right of the city of Durango. The rest of the trails to the right and below Raider Ridge are all part of the extensive Telegraph Trails Network. Some of the city trails, which are also featured on individual maps, are in the upper left-hand corner of this map in smaller scale.

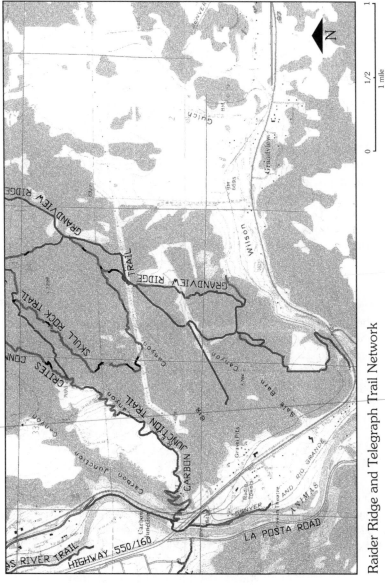

Raider Ridge and Telegraph Trail Network

Perins Peak

Distance: *5 miles (round trip)*
Starting elevation: *6,641 feet*
Elevation gain: *1,699 feet*
High point: *8,340 feet*
Rating: *Difficult*
Time allowed: *3 to 4 hours*
Maps: *7.5'Durango West; San Juan National Forest*

Perins Peak is included in the area restricted by the Colorado Division of Wildlife in order to protect an endangered species, the peregrine falcon, as well as big-game species whose young are born in this area. Human traffic is not permitted from November 15 to July 15. But this is good hiking, and it's worth waiting for the open period. Also, it has the advantage of starting right out from the city limits.

The first part is quite easy, but the last thousand feet of altitude gain are difficult due to steepness and slippery conditions. It is a good vigorous hike and is rewarding for the exercise it provides and for the nice view of both the La Plata Mountains and Durango from the top.

To start, take Twenty-Second Street west off Main Street in Durango. In a couple of blocks, Twenty-Second turns south and climbs Crestview Mesa. At the top, it turns west again and becomes Montview Parkway. Follow it to Glenisle, where you should turn left (south). After one block, turn right on Leyden Street, follow it west until it ends, park at the end, and begin hiking west near the drainage past one last house. There is a well-defined trail following a small stream (fortunately, it is dry most of the time) and crossing it several times. Follow this trail upstream, northwest. At about one-half mile upstream, the trail leaves the stream and climbs a steep ridge of gray Mancos shale. This point is not marked, but it is crucial to find, since farther on you will have to climb out through brush and steep hillsides. Because some people do hike on upstream a ways, a trail is visible here.

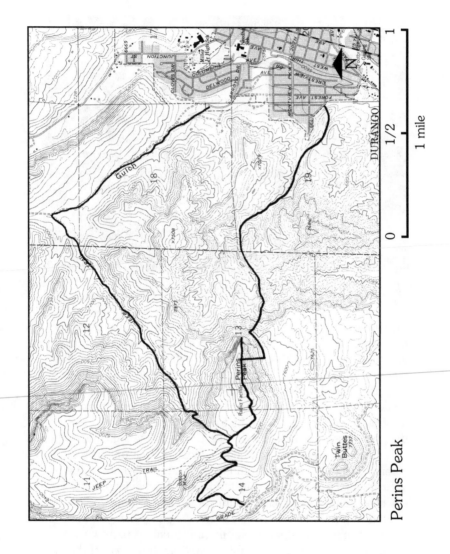

Perins Peak

On Perins Peak after crossing the hazardous gully.

The turnoff can be recognized thus: there is a little flat place on the west side of the stream where the stream makes a turn east and then sharply back west. The shale ridge rises out of this flat place. If you look up it (west), you should be able to see the trail. The trail rises sharply at first and contours around this ridge in a general westerly direction toward the face of Perins Peak. Perins itself has a distinctive profile. Its top has a sharp, pointed cliff that faces east and looks down over Durango like a guardian.

One-half mile along the ridge brings you to a trail division where one branch turns left and leads south up Hogsback Ridge. Your trail goes on west toward the face of Perins. On your left will be a steep shale hillside leading down into Evergreen Valley; on your right will be a tangle of brush. At one point, you have to traverse a bit of the steep shale; there is usually a narrow path (six to ten inches wide) along this area. Sometimes bits of the path have slipped away, and you simply have to dig in your boots for a foothold. Fortunately, the shale is usually soft. Just beyond this, you swing northwest and ascend toward a large shale rib coming down from the peak. There is a well-defined path in this area on up the rib. There are several of these ribs. The correct one ascends to a point just to the left of the pointed cliff. If you are on the correct rib, you will come to one last lonely piñon tree hanging on to life in the shale. At thirty to forty yards above the tree you leave the path and start making your own way; there is no more significant path the rest of the way though you may strike some game trails that are useful for a way.

At the turnoff point above the tree, go left and traverse the steep sides of a shale gully. Into the gully and out the far side is less than fifty yards, but it is the most hazardous part of the hike, for a loosened footstep could give you a long ride to the bottom of the shale. Fortunately, some brush is available for grasping along the climb out, where it is steepest.

Once over the far edge of the gully, you will find yourself in a mixture of rocks and some brush. This is a slow area but not dangerous. Pick your way along a contour toward the base of the cliff at its southeast corner. This appears to be a cliff of mud and shale with some ominous cracks in it. I like to stay a little below this. Once beyond the cliff, going southwest, you can turn back north for the final assault. You will have about 500 feet of steep ascent over big rocks and through some brush. Stay west of the cliffs some fifty feet or more for safety's sake and for more openness in the brush.

At the top of the rocks is a sandstone wall ten to thirty feet straight up. I have a favorite old dead tree that I can climb easily in three well-placed steps to a low bench on this wall. Once over this, it is an easy 100 yards through oak brush to the top. If you miss my tree, you can contour farther west around the base of the wall to a usable break in it. Now you are above the pointed cliff face and are ready to collect your reward for the effort you have expended. Go east from your top-out point to the rocky point. But exercise care as you go out there, remembering how far up you are.

The actual high point is an easy quarter-mile west of the face cliff. Since it is bare, you can get fine views in all directions. Also, you will find near the top two objects that look like large blank billboards. They are microwave reflectors.

The mileage and time listed in the heading presuppose a return over the approach route. But there are a couple of other options, one north and one west. Either one will leave you some distance from your starting point. The north route will leave you a two-mile hike back through town if you have not left a car there. The west route will leave you about six miles out of town. Both are interesting routes and worth the trouble of putting another car at the terminal point.

I will describe both routes, the north one first. Start down over an old four-wheel-drive road, now abandoned, that reaches the top of the peak from the west. Follow this down one-half mile to where it just begins to level out. For the north route, turn right at this point down the head of the first drainage that you reach from the top of the peak. This is an open meadow area. There is a trail, but the beginning of it tends to be grassed over. Hike down this trail and turn right at the edge of the trees. This should put you on the remains of an old road that zigzags down a canyon northeasterly. This route is not as steep as the one leading up the mountain. It is well defined down through the canyon and tall timber. The price of an easier trail is a longer distance. From the top back to the edge of town by this route is four miles versus the two and one-half miles on the climb route.

At the end of the canyon you will come to more open territory. Currently, the trail swings east and soon crosses a fence into private property where there is a road that goes on into town a mile away. This development is called Rockridge, and its developer is friendly to hikers. He has built a hiking trail to traverse the full length of this property, heading toward the gate of the Division of Wildlife property, which lies on the route of an old four-wheel-drive road. This is north 300 yards from where the trail swings east toward the fence. There is no path for this distance, but the gate is about due north across mostly open meadow with a few trees near the beginning. A better route is northeast toward the nearest houses. Cross the fence and take the road to the left; it soon turns mostly to the east. If you do it right, you should strike the developer's trail; if you don't, you are still okay, because the street will bring you out at essentially the same place. The distance to the corner of Clovis and Borrego streets (formerly the edge of town) is one mile along the trail; it is a picturesque route following the edge of an arroyo, avoiding most of the vehicular traffic.

For the westerly route, come down from the top the same way. A quarter mile beyond the north route turnoff, the road divides in a flat area. Take the left fork here downhill. You will need to watch closely for the beginning of this left fork since it has been bulldozed full of brush and dirt.

Hikers on the Dry Creek to Durango Trail with the north point of Perins Peak behind them.

An interesting feature of this route is the site of Perins City and the Boston Coal Mine. About a quarter-mile down from the road divide, you come to another level spot. Go to the northwest end to find the site of the town and the mine.

No buildings remain here, but the place was once very busy, being one of the largest coal mines in southwest Colorado. It was active during the first quarter of the twentieth century. A railroad wound its way up the mountainside to carry out the coal.

You could hike out the old right-of-way, but it is very long due to the gradual grade that the train could tolerate. The recommended route down from here is to go west and a little south over the side of this mountain. This will be bushwhacking through some oak brush, but you can go around most of it. There are 600 feet more of descent. Many summer lupines bloom profusely on this hillside. You will have to cross a fence or two, but the land is public on both sides—some of it U.S. land and some belongs to the state. You should end up on Dry Creek Road just to the north of Lightner Creek Road, one and one-half miles north of U.S. Highway 160.

Perins Peak is usually thought of as the point already
described, but the same massif actually peaks out again at the
north end, a mile west and two miles north of the first peak. For
hikers who would like to devote an entire day to this uplift, the
northern peak could be added. This means turning north at the
spot where you are directed to start down from the meadow over
the old jeep road toward Perins City and the mine. Instead of
going down over the bulldozed barrier, turn right (north) and look
for an old trail that is likely to be faint or nonexistent in some
places and clear in others. The north end is two miles away, but
most of the route is not timbered; therefore, it is easy to find
your way as long as you are gradually rising through the
meadow. The northern peak is actually higher than the main
one; at 8,682 feet, it is 342 feet higher. Furthermore, it is just
as dramatic but in a different way. It juts out for nearly a hundred
yards over the valley to the north. Here it narrows to a sharp
blade of bare rock with three distinctive levels—a view not seen
by many but well worth the extra effort. You can see this point
from below at an opening in the timber on the hike from Dry
Creek to Durango. This is at the highest point on that trail just
one mile in from the west end.

Dry Fork Loop

Distance: *9 miles*
Starting elevation: *7,300 feet*
Elevation gain: *1,000 feet*
High point: *8,300 feet (northwest corner)*
Rating: *Moderate*
Time allowed: *3.5 to 4.5 hours*
Maps: *7.5' Durango West; San Juan National Forest; Durango
Area Recreation Map*

This is a new loop trail that takes advantage of the Colorado
Trail for the upper part of the loop. It starts along a drainage,
then splits and moves up through big timber.

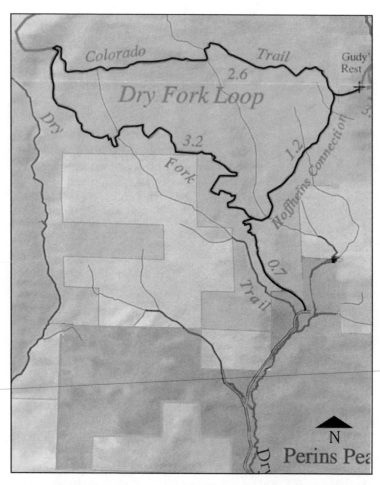

Colorado Trail

Gudy's Rest

2.6

Dry Fork Loop

Dry

3.2

Fork

1.2

Hoffheins Connection

3.

0.7

Trail

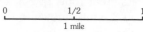

N

Perins Pea

Dry

Dry Fork Loop

0   1/2   1

1 mile

To take this hike, go up Lightner Creek Road and then take the Dry Fork Road as described in "Dry Fork to Durango." Instead of parking just below the cattleguard, go straight ahead across it and on about a half mile more to the first left turnoff. The trailhead is a hundred yards in here with lots of parking space.

This is a very busy trail in nice weather and is used by hikers, bikers, and horseback riders, with bikers predominant. It is a pleasant hike on good trail and is shady most of the way. A sign at the trailhead shows the route and describes the entire loop as being 9 miles. My map gives segment mileage that adds up to 8.4 miles. Maybe it just seems longer when you do the whole loop at once.

The route goes northwest seven-tenths mile, rising gradually to the split. The right side goes mostly north with some switchbacks as it becomes steeper. This section is called Hoffheins Connection; it reaches the Colorado Trail in 1.2 miles. This is the northeast corner of the loop. Just east a bit on the Colorado Trail is a spot worthy of this slight detour. It is called Gudy's Rest. It is a beautiful overlook where you can admire the continuing Colorado Trail far below in Junction Creek Valley as it nears its Durango termination. A concrete resting bench has been placed here where presumably Gudy Gaskill took a well-deserved rest near the finish of the great work she had done in organizing and pushing through to completion this enormous project connecting Denver to Durango by foot trail, a distance of 474 miles.

Back at the intersection, follow the Colorado Trail west 2.6 miles to the third leg of the loop, which is called Dry Fork Trail. The Colorado Trail turns north here, headed toward Kennebec Pass. Your route goes southeasterly down Dry Fork, winding its way 3.2 miles down to the union with Hoffheins Connection and thence back to the beginning in seven-tenths mile.

Perins Peak Wildlife Area—
Becker Tract

This is a little-used area west of Perins Peak that is detached from it. It is an elevated spot located between Lightner Creek and U.S. Highway 160 west of Durango. Although it is close to Durango, difficult access and zero population make it an unknown place for most Durango residents. It is therefore a good place for hikers who want some solitude while wandering through nature's offerings. It is heavily wooded with big pines and some oak.

Unless you want to climb a steep mountainside through big trees and brush, there is only one access—a very rough four-wheel-drive road, the first mile of which is through private property (but legal to use).

Access to this area is four and one-half miles west of the U.S. 160 bridge over the Animas River in southern Durango, or one mile west of the Lightner Creek turnoff from U.S. 160. Here you will see a little road on the right through an open gate. It is on the east end of an old mining spot. This begins the four-wheel-drive area. If you have only a two-wheel-drive vehicle, park just inside the gate to the side of the road; this road becomes difficult very quickly. The road goes up above some old coal mines for one mile to the boundary of the wildlife area and is rough all the way. A sign is posted here to identify the area. Most of the roads inside are better than the approach road, but there are still some very bad spots, necessitating the use of a four-wheel-drive. The first road to the right goes for a half mile to a turnaround. It is better to hike this than drive it. There are trees close on each side but some good overlooks on the right down to the highway. Back on the main road, going north, you soon come to another right-hand road that is fairly good but that is currently blocked for vehicles by a steel cable. It still makes a good hike that goes east to near the dropoff; it then swings to the north side and goes back to the west, higher up to the main road. This is a good two-mile hike.

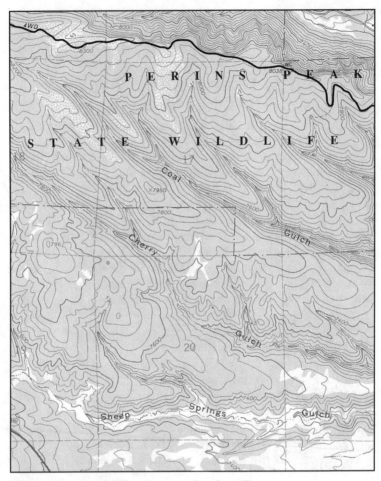

Perins Peak Wildlife Area — Becker Tract

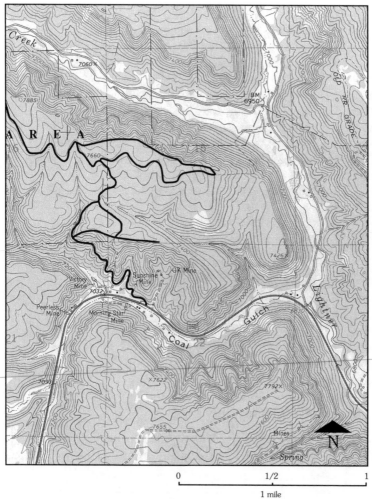

The main road now curves to the west and, after negotiating some turns and hills, settles down to a slow, gradual rise mostly along the top of the ridge. You can drive about two more miles to a barrier for cars. The hiking trail goes on for more than a mile. The drivable part, along with the hike-only part, would make a good longer hike, most of it fairly easy. The ridge becomes quite narrow in places, making you feel on top of the world and affording some nice views on the right several hundred feet down into Lightner Creek with its many houses, and on north to Barnroof Point and northwest to the La Platas. There is an open view to the south of some lower hills.

I enjoy the feeling of remoteness and solitude available here, even though you are not far from town. On a nice summer weekend afternoon, you may meet other people, but not many.

You can only return by the same road you came up.

Log Chutes Trails

Distance: *Two loops, 4.7 miles and 6.3 miles*
Starting elevation: *7,400 feet*
Elevation gain: *600 feet*
High point: *8,000 feet*
Rating: *Easy*
Time allowed: *2.5 to 4.5 hours*
Maps: *7.5' Durango West; San Juan National Forest; Durango Area Recreation Map*

This is a group of trails not far from Durango in the Junction Creek area. The San Juan Mountains Association is a private auxiliary group designed to promote good relations between the Forest Service and the public. The group also does projects to help out these lands when federal funding is inadequate. One of their main fund-raising projects is the sponsoring of a unique race over the Log Chutes Trails. The principal recreational uses of the trails are hiking, biking, and horseback riding. This race creates teams of three people representing each of these activities. There

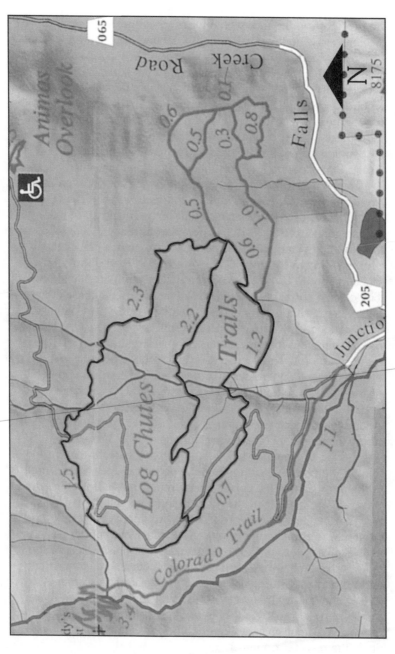

Log Chutes Trail

are two loops in the race with a lot of same trail in them. The
shorter loop is done by the hikers (or joggers, as each participant
decides for himself/herself); the longer loop is assigned to the
bikers and the horse riders. All ages and both sexes participate.
Because this covers a wide variety of abilities, the winning team
is not determined by speed, but by the best prediction of the total
time of the entire team. It is a well-organized, fun activity. It also
helps these three groups of trail users to think about sharing and
cooperation on the trails. These two loops are featured in this
description, although the trails may be combined in other ways.

To reach the trailhead, take West 25th Street off Main Street
across from the fairgrounds entrance. This soon becomes
Junction Creek Road, changing again at the boundary of the
national forest to F.S. 171. The boundary is marked by a cattle
guard; at this same point, the paved road becomes gravel and
soon turns into a twisting, climbing mountain road. From the
boundary, go up about a mile and a half, where you should be
able to see a corral on a left-hand side road. This is considered
the trailhead, although other areas can be used to start the hike.
Good parking is available near the corral. According to the map,
the trail starts out to the southeast, paralleling the main road just
to the south of it. This section is level to slightly downhill. At
seven-tenths mile, it crosses over the road and starts a long uphill
section that has some turns and one long, straight section. At
1.8 miles, the trail splits, with the shorter route turning sharply
left and the longer route going straight ahead; it also turns left
shortly in a general northwesterly direction. In 2.3 miles, it
crosses F.S. 171 and stays beyond it, curving back to the starting
point at the corral. The shorter route doesn't cross F.S. 171 until
just before reaching the corral. These routes mostly follow roads,
some that are now closed to vehicles and some that are still in
use. There are several hundred feet of rise in both routes, but the
long route rises higher than the other. In fact, the shorter route is
relatively flat before it starts to descend to the finish. Most of the
trail is in big timber, but there are a few spots where you can see
out to distant views, especially along the western, descending
part. In addition to the two loops used for the race course, there
is an eastern loop of about three and one-half miles. Therefore,
you could sort out several different hikes from the whole group.
(Study the map for options.)

Hikes up and on Missionary Ridge

Haflin Creek Trail

Distance: *3.5 miles (one way)*
Starting elevation: *6,620 feet*
Elevation gain: *3,080 feet*
High point: *9,700 feet*
Rating: *Moderate*
Time allowed: *3 hours*
Maps: *7.5' Durango East; San Juan National Forest*

For those who like to hike in deep woods, Haflin Canyon makes a good half-day hike. It takes you up from the Animas Valley through nearly 3,000 feet of ascent, almost always among trees. This hike also illustrates very well the different climatic zones and the associated forestation. At the bottom, you start among piñon, junipers, and oak brush. Soon you reach a level of ponderosa pine; this gives way to quaking aspen and the beginning of spruce and fir.

Haflin is a small creek in a deep and rugged canyon that breaks through the west, steep side of Missionary Ridge. You start near the creek, rise high above it, later come even with it, cross it, and finally rise through an open brushy area to the top of the ridge above the stream source. In this brushy area, you can get good views to the west of the river valley from which you have come and to the La Platas beyond.

To take this trail, leave Durango east on Thirty-Second Street off Main Street about 1.2 miles to a left turn on East Animas Road. At just over five miles up this road, you should see a sign (on the east side of the road) for Haflin Creek Trail. Off-the-road parking is available here.

The trail starts off nearly flat in an easterly direction but soon launches into a series of climbing switchbacks, some of them a

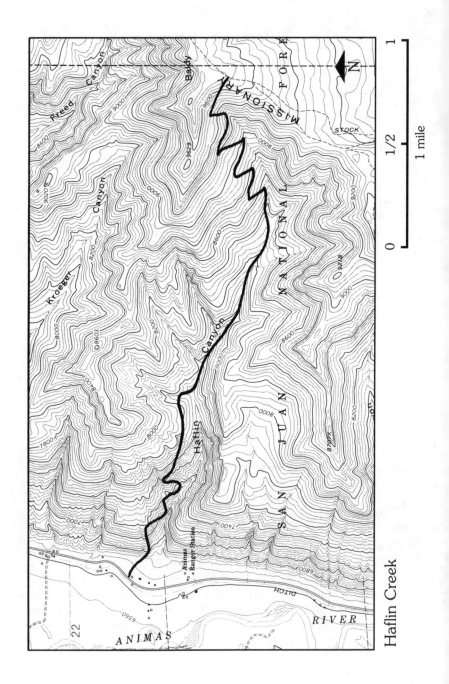

Haflin Creek

Haflin Creek.

bit steep. The first one is a bit obscure; it switches sharply to the left and up a few yards before reaching a little windowless building that sits at the mouth of the canyon. The trail eventually parallels the stream that is cascading and falling far below. The trail is easy to follow most of the way until the stream rises up to it where there is some old flooding debris in a fairly flat area. This is the one place where the trail is sometimes not quite clear, but at the upper end of this flat area, it begins to rise up the hillside again out the north side after crossing and recrossing the creek. Not far above this you come out into a steep, brushy area and, in a series of switchbacks, arrive at the top of the ridge where this trail joins the Missionary Ridge Trail in the aspen.

This is listed as a half-day hike, but you could lengthen it by going either north or south on the Missionary Ridge Trail. This is why distance and time for this hike are listed as one-way. Returning on Haflin Creek Trail would complete a half-day.

South on the Missionary Ridge Trail hiking is good for a couple of miles, but beyond that the trail soon descends to private property, causing an access problem.

North on this trail soon brings you to the top of Baldy Mountain (9,805 feet). Beyond this point lie several possible descent routes. Within five and one-half miles are three easterly descents and one westerly descent. The westerly descent is Stevens Creek. The easterly descents are in order with mileages from Baldy: First Fork (1.5 miles), Red Creek (2.6 miles), Shearer Creek (5.5 miles). All of these lead down to Florida Road or other roads leading to Florida Road. All these trails will be discussed separately.

No part of this hike is difficult, but it is rated moderate because of the relatively large amount of altitude gain. It is well worth the effort because of the variations of trees, the wildflowers, and the changing vistas.

Stevens Creek Trail

Distance: *16.5 miles (round trip)*
Starting elevation: *6,660 feet*
Elevation gain: *3,300 feet*
High point: *9,960 feet*
Rating: *Difficult (only because of the long distance)*
Time allowed: *8 to 11 hours*
Maps: *7.5′Hermosa; San Juan National Forest*

This hike, like the Haflin Creek hike, is up the west side of Missionary Ridge to the Missionary Ridge Trail across the top, but it is much longer because the route is less direct and because the Ridge Trail at the top swings east quite a distance. There is nothing difficult about it except its length. The steepest part is at the beginning, where you gain 1,000 feet in a little more than a mile, but even this is over good trail. After that there are few steep areas. The route follows constructed trail and several old mountain roads, most of them closed to cars and trucks. It is a good way to get some vigorous exercise and enjoy beautiful mountain scenery that is not available from the highways. This trail was not included in previous editions of this guide because it was so easy to lose in several places, especially through a logging area. But it has been rebuilt and partly rerouted recently. It is now a very good trail and is easy to follow, with signs at all key points of intersections with other trails. It passes through big-timber areas of pine, aspen, fir, and spruce, as well as through some open meadowland with streams in the valleys. Very little of it is rocky. The hike is pleasant for its full length and therefore is a nice all-day hike.

The trail lies several miles north of Durango. You can go up the East Animas Road (C.R. 250) from Florida Road or the east end of 32nd Street all the way to the trailhead. Perhaps easier, you can go north out of Durango on U.S. 550 to Trimble Lane, six and one-half miles north of 32nd Street, and a mile south of

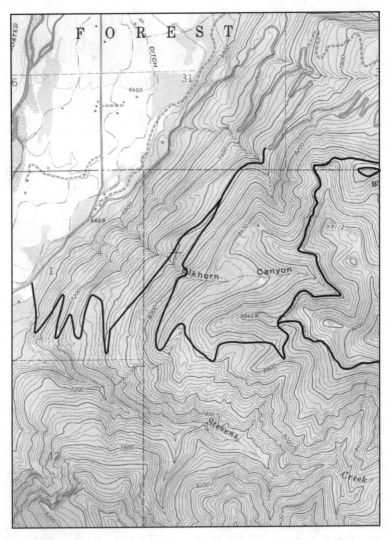

Stevens Creek

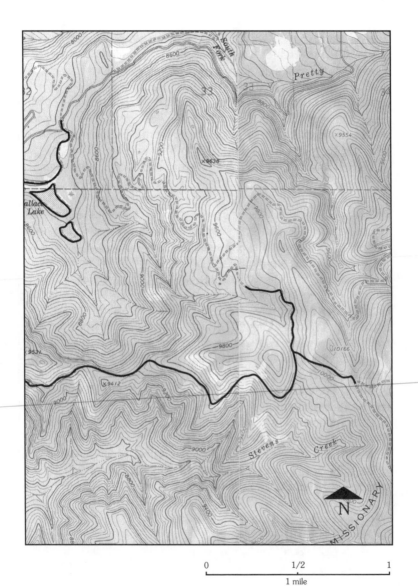

0   1/2   1

1 mile

Hermosa Village. Go east on Trimble Lane over the river, then left on East Animas for about three and a half miles. The trailhead is on the east side of the road and is a little hard to see, as it is located under big trees between houses. If you miss it, turn around at the beginning of Missionary Ridge Road and go back four-tenths mile. Parking is available for a few cars. There is also a sign for Stevens Creek Trail, but it is on the side of a big tree in from the road and is faded enough to be missed easily.

There is a way to split this trail into two shorter hikes, but unfortunately, the longer section is still 14.7 miles long. It does put nearly a third of the total altitude gain in the short hike. To do this, drive up the Missionary Ridge Road 3.7 miles to a place where there is a particularly sharp switchback after a long, more straight part. There are many switchbacks on this road, so it is important to find the right one. Look for a little road on the right that goes a short distance to a dirt barrier. A few cars can park here. A connecting trail goes beyond the barrier and in six-tenths mile reaches the Stevens Creek Trail, where it makes a major switchback in front of you. There is a wire gate between the two trails that appears to be left open most of the time. Here you can choose to go down to the Stevens Creek trailhead in 2.8 miles or up to the junction with the Missionary Ridge Trail in 14.7 miles. If you go up, you will cut off a third of the altitude gain but not much of the scenery.

At the junction with Missionary Ridge, the trail goes below the top on the west side; therefore, there is no view across to the valley below on the east side. If you want that view, you can go either right or left on that trail, but it will be more than a half mile in either direction to the top.

Wallace Lake

Distance: *1 mile (round trip)*
Starting elevation: *8,200 feet*
Elevation gain: *200 feet*
High point: *8,400 feet*
Rating: *Easy*
Time allowed: *1 hour*
Maps: *7.5'Hermosa; San Juan National Forest*

This is a very easy hike in a nice, secluded area (except during hunting season). It is located well up on the west side of Missionary Ridge and is surrounded by big trees, mostly aspen. The hike itself is short, but the hiking area is several miles from Durango. Still, it is a pleasant drive.

The trail is reached via the East Animas and Missionary Ridge roads. From Durango, take Thirty-Second Street east off the north end of Main Street. Thirty-Second runs into and stops at East Animas Road (CR250). Turn left on it (north), and follow it nine and one-half miles to where Missionary Ridge Road branches off to the right, uphill. People approaching from the north can turn off U.S. Highway 550 at Baker's Bridge Road. Follow this road across the Animas River and south to Missionary Ridge Road, which will be a sharp left turn back and uphill.

Missionary Ridge Road is gravel and often plagued by a washboard effect. It also climbs steeply up a series of many switchbacks. So it is a slow road, but it yields fine views of the Animas Valley from a higher and higher perspective. Westward across the valley, the Hermosa Cliffs and La Plata Mountains grow ever more impressive as you continue to climb.

After climbing Missionary Ridge Road for a little less than six miles, you come to the Wallace Lake turnoff. There should be ample parking here. Actually, four-wheel-drive vehicles can go on to the lake, but the hike is pleasant and short. Shortly after the trail begins, the road branches. Go to the right, and you will soon

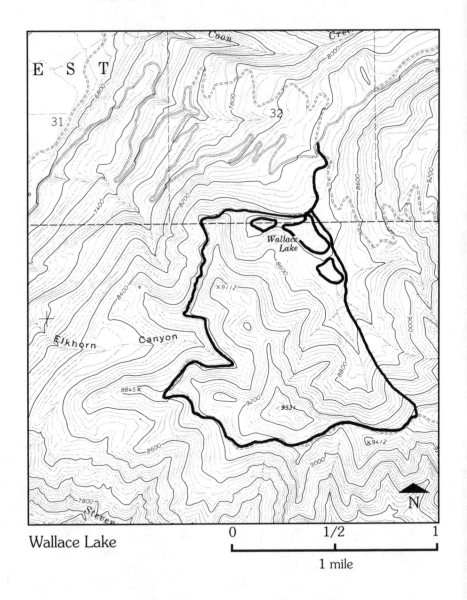

Wallace Lake

be at the lake. Actually, there are two other small lakes. You reach the main lake first with the others to the right and left of it. All of these lakes are shallow. In dry years, they sometimes dry up completely. Whether there is water or not, it is a peaceful and lovely spot. During the fall, it is surrounded by golden-clad aspen.

Those who want a more vigorous hike can follow the jeep road on around to the right alongside two of the lakes. It twists and turns and climbs another three and one-half miles up to 9,500 feet. It passes through big timber and a couple of open spots. At the 9,500 foot spot, you will be on a ridge dividing the Stevens Creek and Wallace Lake drainages. The short route back to Wallace is one mile northwest, but you must bushwhack down the steep side of the basin, following the creek to the uppermost of the three lakes.

Mountain View Crest

Distance: *9 to 10 miles (round trip)*
Starting elevation: *11,480 feet (10,600 feet)*
Elevation gain: *1,518 feet (2,398 feet)*
High point: *12,998 feet*
Rating: *Moderate (long and high but not difficult)*
Time allowed: *7 to 8 hours*
Maps: *7.5'Mountain View Crest; San Juan National Forest*

This hike lies northeast of Durango over a number of miles of gravel road (usually somewhat rough) and a short distance of four-wheel-drive road. So access is slow, but the end of the trail offers some of the most fantastic scenery in Colorado. I am going to suggest some variations on the terminal area that will vary time, mileage, and altitude. The statistics given above are about medium for the options. Once in the area, you will want to take advantage of the full range of views. I have made this hike in a half-day, but a long, full day is much better to allow you to get a good exposure to its riches.

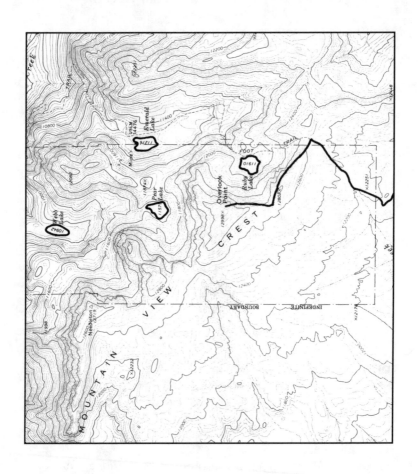

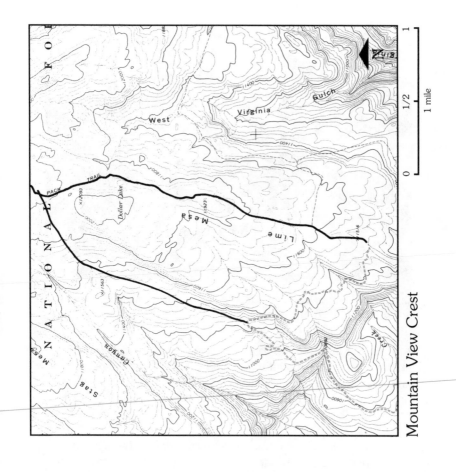

Mountain View Crest

Lunch stop on the way to Mountain View Crest; Lime Mesa is on the left, Dollar Lake is just ahead.

To find this area, go to Thirty-Second Street off the north end of Main Street in Durango. Follow Thirty-Second east to its end (1.2 miles) at East Animas Road (CR250). Follow this road north nine and one-half miles to where Missionary Ridge Road separates off uphill to the right. This is a climbing gravel road with many switchbacks. Follow it nineteen miles to where Henderson Lake Road branches off to the right. This is a four-wheel-drive road about four miles long, but two-wheel-drive vehicles can make half or more of it when the road is dry. The road ends at the wilderness barrier, where you will find plenty of parking space. At this point, hike straight north along the east side of Lime Mesa, following the old jeep road past Dollar Lake to a saddle at the east end of Mountain View Crest.

Those who must stop farther back with two-wheel-drive cars will have to hike an extra mile or more and gain an extra 800 feet. They need not hike all the way to the wilderness barrier. Where the road goes northeast and turns sharply back south, climbing, hikers should head straight north along the west side of Lime Mesa. In 1.3 miles you come to the north end of it; the trail is pretty good along most of this route. At the north end of

Pidgeon and Turret peaks across Needle Creek Valley from Mountain View Crest.

the mesa you are at timberline; swing right here across the tundra. A quarter-mile beyond, you should intersect the old jeep road described above. Take it left another one and one-half miles to the saddle at the east end of Mountain View Crest.

At the saddle you begin to see the dramatic views, but they are even better if you climb left a quarter-mile to the top of the first rise (12,802 feet). The second rise, a quarter-mile beyond, is called Overlook Point, and it stands at 12,998 feet.

The drama is below and beyond—in the form of four beautiful lakes. To the right and below Overlook Point lies, first, Ruby Lake, and a little farther north and lower, Emerald Lake. To the left and down are Pear Lake and Webb Lake. All of these provide excellent trout fishing. To go down to them commits you to an overnight stay, for they are farther away than they first appear. Overlook Point is the only place from which all four lakes can be seen. The first top reveals only Ruby and Emerald.

But the view down to the lakes is only the start of the scenery. Far below them is Needle Creek—too far down to see—but across Needle Canyon and abruptly above rise Pidgeon and Turret peaks. Pidgeon is higher at 13,972 feet and drops a sheer 1,000 feet on its east side to the saddle between it and Turret, which rises up the other side to 13,835 feet. These two miss being fourteeners by a small margin, but there is no more dramatic view in the San Juan Mountains. Viewing the east face of Pidgeon can send shivers up and down your back, let alone standing on its top.

There is still more to see, if you have time.

Go back to the original saddle overlooking Ruby Lake. From this point, pick up a trail going east, and hike three miles. You can end up climbing north off the trail to the top of Mount Kennedy. It has a double top, with the farthest being the highest (13,125 feet). Either top will give about the same view.

The view here is to the north into Chicago Basin, surrounded by the Needles—three fourteeners. They are, from west to east, Eolus, Sunlight, and Windom. This is one of the most popular backpacking areas in the state. People ride the Durango-Silverton train to Needleton and hike nine miles up Needle Creek to Chicago Basin, where a base camp can be established for climbing all three peaks.

While the three fourteeners, in my opinion, are not quite as dramatic as Pidgeon, they are certainly powerful and majestic. This is truly wilderness area par excellence. Behind these mountains you get glimpses of the tops of other peaks showing through the saddles.

By this time, you should know that I have described more than the mileage given in the heading. It would be a very long hike to cover all of this and get back to your car in one day, so you may have to make a choice whether you do the east or west side from the saddle. In any case, the return to the starting point will repeat the approach route.

Burnt Timber Trail

Distance: *6.5 miles (round trip)*
Starting elevation: *8,500 feet*
Elevation gain: *2,500 feet*
High point: *11,000 feet*
Rating: *Easy*
Time allowed: *2.5 to 3.5 hours*
Maps: *7.5' Lemon Reservoir; 7.5' Needle Mountains; San Juan National Forest*

Some hikers may think that the easy rating for this trail is underrated because of the climbing, but there is nothing difficult about any part of it. It just goes steadily upward at a good incline and requires a slower pace and more rest for some hikers than other easy trails.

This is a rewarding hike, for it traverses genuine backcountry and stays near the rugged Florida River canyon. The east side of this canyon presents a high, imposing wall of timber and rock. Most of this hike is in the trees along the base of the east side of Missionary Ridge, but there are frequent views eastward through the trees. The last mile shuts off the eastward view while passing through a high-altitude open, but steep, meadow.

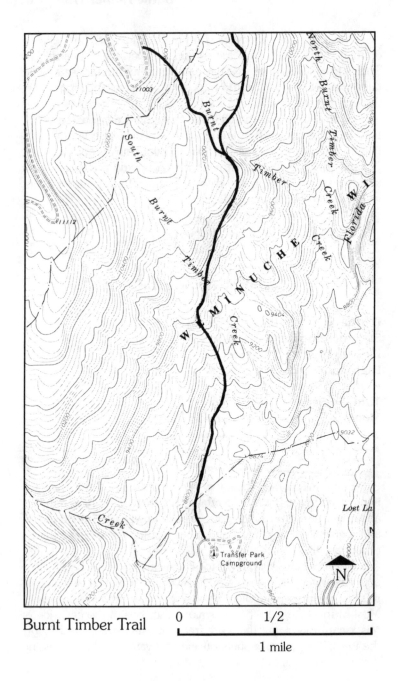

Burnt Timber Trail

0   1/2   1

1 mile

To find the trailhead from Durango, take East Third Avenue north to its end, and turn right (northeast) on Florida Road. Follow this out of town thirteen miles to Lemon Lake Road. This spot is easily recognized: The main road here turns right at a ninety-degree angle around a little country store and crosses the Florida River. Lemon Lake Road goes straight on at the turn and is gravel. A couple of miles up this road you come to the dam, behind which is impounded beautiful Lemon Lake or, more properly, Lemon Reservoir. This is an irrigation supply filled by melting winter snows. It is peaceful and inviting, nestled as it is at the base of high wooded hills on each side. Lemon is a favorite fishing and picnicking spot with several good sites along its banks.

To reach the trail, drive along the side of the lake and two miles beyond its north end. Here you cross a cattleguard; one road goes straight on up Miller Mountain, but you should turn left into the Florida Campground. In a quarter-mile you cross Florida River, then immediately turn left. There are two left options here; the sharpest left is only a camping loop. Take the other one. It winds on around south, west, and north again for a mile and ends up in Transfer Park Campground, tucked into a flat spot next to the river. This is an excellent and secluded camping spot.

Plenty of parking space is available where you first enter the campground, at the northwest corner. The trail begins at the north side of this area.

The trail is a good one—it is well maintained and easy to follow. It is used by horseback riders as well as hikers. The three and one-fourth miles (one way) given in the heading takes you to the old Burnt Timber Road along the top of Missionary Ridge. Some may wish to turn back shortly after entering the meadow instead of climbing on up to the road, which is a mile farther and 800 feet higher; you would then have to follow the trail still farther to get good views of surrounding peaks. Others may want to go even farther, for the trail continues, eventually coming to a crossover to Lime Mesa Trail west and north or going on to a turn eastward that takes you to Durango City Reservoir, some thirteen miles from Transfer Park. This is beautiful country but carries you into backpacking instead of day-hiking distances.

The projected 6.5-mile hike presupposes returning to Transfer Park from Burnt Timber Road by the same route as you came.

Red Creek Trail

Distance: *7 miles (round trip)*
Starting elevation: *8,080 feet*
Elevation gain: *1,519 feet*
High point: *9,599 feet*
Rating: *Easy, except the last half mile*
Time allowed: *3 to 4 hours*
Maps: *7.5'Rules Hill; 7.5'Lemon Reservoir; 7.5'Hermosa;*
7.5'Durango East (the trail goes through the corners of
these four maps); San Juan National Forest

Red Creek Trail is a lovely hike any time the snow is not too deep, but it is especially good on a warm summer day; for most of the way it follows a nice gurgling stream at the bottom of a narrow canyon in the shade of big fir, spruce, and aspen trees. The trail is easy to follow. It climbs quite gradually for three miles, then, steeply, up a series of switchbacks the last half-mile to the top of Missionary Ridge.

To get to Red Creek from Durango, take East Third Avenue north to its end and turn right on Florida Road. Follow this road northeast out of town ten miles to a left turn uphill (north), where there should be a sign reading "Colvig Silver Camps—1 mile." This is a good gravel road for that distance. At the Camps, you get the impression that the road is about to end, but it does not; continue north, right through the Camps for another mile. This second mile is much narrower and rougher. At the end of the second mile, turn left off the road. Currently there is a sign marked "Red Creek Trail" at the turnoff. Just after turning you will come to a good open spot for parking. The trail begins at the west side of this open area.

The quality of the approach road varies. Recently it has been fairly good, but sometimes it is washed out to the point that only four-wheel-drive vehicles can make it all the way to this area. When it is in that condition two-wheel-drives will need to park

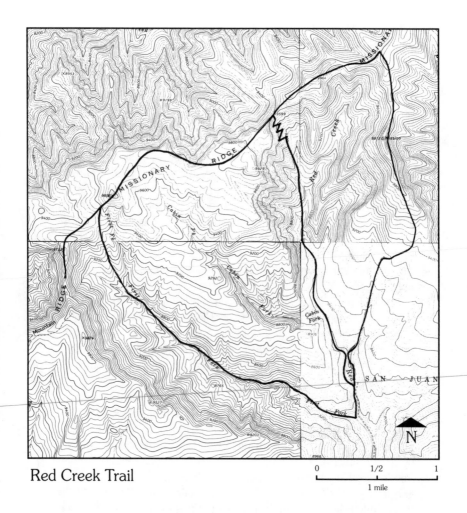

Red Creek Trail

0   1/2   1

1 mile

300 yards short of the turnoff at the bottom of the last hill, which is often washed out and full of big rocks. Anyway, it adds only a short distance to the total hike to have to walk up the hill.

The hike itself, after leaving the road, stays close to the creek, crossing it occasionally, as it gradually rises through the timber. Because the last half-mile to the top is much steeper, those who want a very easy hike could turn around at this point. The steep part, however, is a set of switchbacks and is really not too bad; it is used by horses. In fact, this is a favorite trail for elk hunters in the fall. (Heavy rains in the summer of 1999 channeled out some of the switchbacks in the steep part of the trail near the end. Some of these are a foot and a half or more deep and are also very narrow. In the same places, the summer plant growth got two to three feet tall. For a short distance, this combination makes hiking slow and difficult. But you must go on, for the end is near. Hopefully, this part of the trail will be repaired before long.)

Red Creek Trail terminates in a saddle at the top of the ridge, where it runs into Missionary Ridge Trail. This is a very good trail where Red Creek joins it. For hikers who want to go farther, this trail can be hiked northeast or southwest for some distance. The San Juan National Forest map shows it going south all the way to Florida Road two miles east of Durango.

The distance figure of seven miles given in the trail description at the beginning assumes turning around at the union with the Missionary Ridge Trail. However, this hike can be extended into a good loop hike that brings you back to the starting point by a different route. To take the loop go northeast along Missionary Ridge. The trail begins to climb gradually right away and in a short distance shifts to a steep climb of 350 feet. At the top of this it levels off in a grove of big trees. In a short distance (a few hundred yards) a good trail (currently unmarked) swings off the main trail to the right (southeast); take this for the return. It starts out level but begins shortly to descend gradually.

Once on the right trail, it is fairly easy to follow, though the last time I was over it there was some need of maintenance due to aspen logs that had fallen across it.

The trail follows a very narrow ridge between the main branch of Red Creek and West Fork of Shearer Creek for over a mile. Although this ridge is well timbered, it is a delightful hiking area due to the fine views down each side, especially the Shearer Creek (east) side. You can look down a canyon wall of some 600 feet and across a heavily wooded area for several miles beyond. The last time I was there in the early fall I heard a bull elk bugling in the distance below.

Where the narrow ridge begins to broaden, the trail remains high and close to the Shearer Canyon overlook for another half-mile or more before starting more steeply downhill to the south-west. In less than another half-mile, the trail joins an old logging road and descends in a series of switchbacks for more than another mile to a usable jeep road. In a few hundred yards down this road you should come to the recommended parking place. Just before the last descent the road splits; if you should happen to take the left side and miss the last ridge, never fear, for that side will take you down a steep incline to a small stream; across it, the road turns right and in a short distance also comes back to where you turned in to park. The loop route is less than a mile longer than the round trip over Red Creek Trail.

This loop hike could also be done in reverse, but there is more difficulty following it, for the logging road after you have climbed it a way splits several times. If you do miss the right one, continue uphill northeast to the Shearer Canyon rim and follow the previous directions in reverse. Somewhere along this rim you should be able to find the trail.

Another, longer, loop trip can be taken using the First Fork Trail to climb to Missionary Ridge and then returning via Red Creek Trail. It is about ten miles long, a good day hike. This trail begins a quarter-mile earlier than the Red Creek Trail. It currently has a sign marking its starting point. Coming up the same approach road you turn left and cross the stream before climbing the last hill on the road. There is a sign at the turn marked "First Fork." Begin the trail on the north (uphill) side of a small fenced-in corral. The trail moves west near the stream for more than two miles before emerging into an open meadow that gradually slopes uphill toward the ridge. The trail tends to be hard to track in the meadow, but you should be able to pick it up again by moving uphill to the right at about forty-five degrees from the approach. This will be northerly. There is a cliff to be bypassed. If you do not find the trail you can head anywhere toward the top of the ridge after getting around the cliff. This part is heavily wooded. At the top, turn right on Missionary Ridge Trail through woods and charming meadows and across some easy rises. In about two miles you descend into the small saddle where the Red Creek Trail begins its steep descent down the switchbacks referred to earlier. In three and a half miles this brings you back to the road. A quarter-mile down that you will get back to the First Fork Trail beginning. This loop could also be done in reverse, but at the top of the ridge it is harder to find the beginning of the descent down First Fork Trail.

Shearer Creek Trail

Distance: *11 miles (round trip)*
Starting elevation: *7,560 feet*
Elevation gain: *2,640 feet*
High point: *10,200 feet*
Rating: *Easy, but fairly long*
Time allowed: *4.5 to 6 hours*
Maps: *7.5' Rules Hill; 7.5' Lemon Reservoir; San Juan National Forest*

This is a delightful hike to the top of Missionary Ridge from a southeasterly approach. It starts out climbing a hill above Florida Road and in one mile joins Shearer Creek, which it follows closely almost all the way to the top. The rise is quite gradual most of the way except at the top.

To take the hike from Durango, go east from Main Street downtown on any street to East Third Avenue; follow it north to its end, and turn right at Florida Road. Follow it northeast out of town twelve miles to the beginning of the trail. On the west side is a small turnout and parking area. Just above this you should see a large national forest sign announcing "Shearer Creek Trail." Park here, and begin the hike uphill through a wooden gate. The first two miles are through private property, so you must stay on the trail. However, the forest service has legal

access for the public through this area. The trail is well marked
and is fairly easy to follow uphill through large ponderosa pines.

In one mile, the trail joins the creek and follows it most of
the way to the top of Missionary Ridge. The trail crosses and
recrosses the stream many times. It is a gurgling, pleasant little
stream in the summer and fall and is easily crossed on the rocks.
To hike at the bottom of a deep canyon among big trees is an
enjoyable way to spend a few hours.

In the spring and early summer during the snowmelt, the
stream is higher and much harder to cross, so this trail is not recommended until the major snowpack is gone at levels of 10,000
feet and lower.

The trail joins a road at the top of Missionary Ridge on a
side ridge that reaches southeast fairly level for two miles. The
point of this side ridge overlooks Lemon Lake 2,000 feet below,
but it is heavily wooded, making it hard to see the lake.

The return is by the same route as the climb. There is one
problem on the return—in the last mile after you leave the
stream there are enough cow paths to obscure the main trail.
However, a southeasterly route through here will still get you
down to Florida Road, even if a little off the correct route.

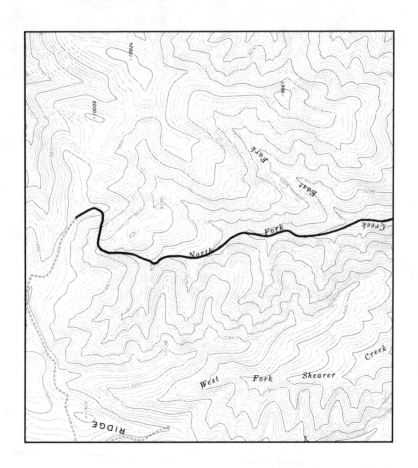

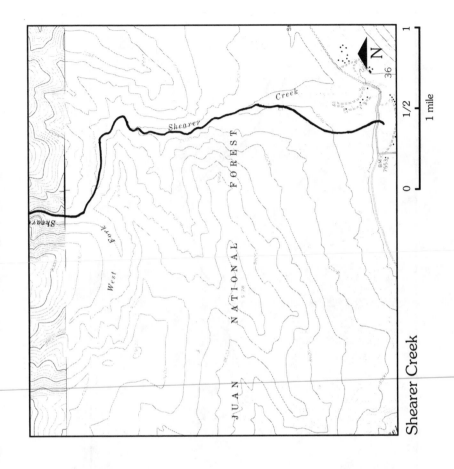

Shearer Creek

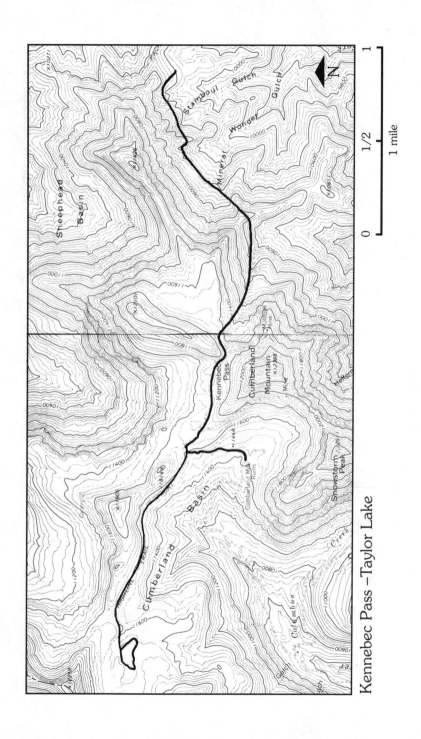

Kennebec Pass – Taylor Lake

La Plata Mountain Climbs

Kennebec Pass–Taylor Lake

Distance: *3 miles (round trip)*
Starting elevation: *10,340 feet*
Elevation gain: *1,420 feet*
High point: *11,760 feet*
Rating: *Moderate*
Time allowed: *2 hours*
Maps: *7.5' Monument Hill; 7.5' La Plata; San Juan*
National Forest

This is a relatively short hike following a long drive on a gravel road, but both the drive and the hike are well worth it. The drive starts at 7,000 feet and slowly winds its way up to the trailhead at 10,340 feet, nearly two-thirds of a mile of altitude gain. It rises through piñon-juniper country, up through ponderosa. Eventually, tall aspen close in on and near the road, along with spruce and fir. During the first ten miles, there are several breaks in the forest that give receding vistas of Durango down in the valley. At about twelve to fifteen miles you come to Rand's Point, where there is a turnout on the left side of the road. Stopping here is well worthwhile, for you look far down into Junction Creek Canyon and across its headwaters to the steep sides of Cumberland Mountain, Snowstorm Peak, and Lewis Mountain. These are among the highest peaks of the east range of the La Platas. Kennebec Pass, the hiking objective, is also visible between Cumberland and a high flat ridge north of it.

To reach the trailhead, take Main Street in Durango to a west turn on Twenty-Fifth Street. In a couple of blocks this curves off to the northwest and becomes Junction Street. Take this out of town, where it becomes Junction Creek Road. The road follows Junction Creek all the way to the national forest boundary. The boundary is easily recognized, for the blacktop stops here with a cattleguard.

Looking down the west ridge below Mount Baker toward La Plata Canyon and across to the western La Plata Mountains.

Check your speedometer at this point. Driving on a gravel road from here on will be slow due to many curves, a steady uphill climb, and often a washboard effect in the surface. (This is great deer and elk country: Your chances of seeing deer are quite good; elk occasionally appear, but they are more apt to stay farther away from the road.) Drive up this road seventeen and one-half miles (allow for some variation in speedometers). At this point you come to a road that turns left. A very large post will be on each side of the road about twenty yards in from Junction Creek Road. Follow this road (south) eight-tenths of a mile to the trailhead. It should be marked "Sliderock Trail" and also "Colorado Trail." The Colorado Trail is coming up from its origin west of Durango; it crosses the road at this point and joins the Sliderock Trail. Here a wide spot a few yards north of the trailhead provides suitable parking space. Your route is uphill at the trail.

When I hiked this trail in mid-August, the wildflowers were abundant; open places displayed great patches of blue larkspur and alpine asters, punctuated with yellow daisies. Farther up were many other kinds of wildflowers. When I hiked this trail in early October, the aspen trees were aflame with gold.

As you near the pass, the trail traverses an open rocky area that yields a view southeastward down the entire Junction Creek Canyon to Durango. The canyon is heavily wooded in dark green; a glance upward toward the pass and Cumberland Mountain shows the light green of tundra above timberline. Every view from this trail is different and beautiful. A quarter-mile farther brings you to the pass. Here the views north and northeast give the best skyline panorama in southwest Colorado. You see the Needles, Twilight and the West Needles, the Grenadiers, Sultan, Engineer, Grizzly, and many others. If you hike 150 yards down the other side of the pass, you see around the west side of the ridge on the north side of the pass, and more of the panorama opens up: Lizard Head, the Wilsons, Dolores Peak, and Lone Cone. Just as you go through the pass there, an unnamed ridge rises on your right (north) 300 feet in a quarter-mile. The view is enhanced even more if you climb it; without this climb the view is excellent but does not come until you get over to the saddle, several hundred yards to the west.

If you are interested in mining history, you can hike a quarter-mile southeast from the pass to an old mine that is in a better stage of preservation than some. It is in an exposed area above timberline, so the views are excellent.

The three miles specified in the heading are based on a return from Kennebec to the starting point. This is a fairly easy hike, though a bit steep.

Taylor Lake can also be included in this hike. It adds another 1.8 miles (one way) to the distance. There is an old four-wheel-drive road, now closed, up to Kennebec from the west. To go to Taylor, take this road down the west side of the pass and a half-mile to where the road turns left and down the hill to Cumberland Basin; at this turn, the trail goes on west to the lake. From the pass to the lake is easy hiking with not much altitude change. There are usually many wildflowers in abundance along this route. Also, if time permits, a side trip down into Cumberland Basin (one-half mile) will be rewarded by even more wildflowers and another mining area.

The trail does go on southwest from Taylor Lake, where it climbs a ridge, drops down into Bear Creek Canyon, and goes up the other side to the pass between Sharkstooth and Centennial Peak. This is described as Sharkstooth Trail and is approached from the west—a much shorter and easier route for that area.

Silver Mountain

Distance: *5.3 miles (round trip)*
Starting elevation: *9,400 feet*
Elevation gain: *3,050 feet*
High point: *12,450 feet*
Rating: *Difficult*
Time allowed: *5 to 6 hours*
Maps: *7.5'La Plata; San Juan National Forest*

Silver Mountain is a vigorous climb on the east ridge of the La Plata Mountains. It is the highest point at the south end of this ridge. Strong parties can do it in a long half-day, perhaps beating the time given above. The first half of the ascent is easy, but the upper half gets quite steep in places. All of the La Plata climbs are rewarded with fine views from the top. The view from Silver is the best from the southeast corner.

The hike starts out of La Plata Canyon. The road is located ten and one-half miles west of Durango off U.S. Highway 160. The canyon road turns north one-third mile west of the Hesperus Post Office. This road is blacktop the first four miles—to Mayday. Beyond this point it is gravel; follow it another five miles. It gets a bit rough, but two-wheel-drives can usually make it all right. The stopping point has room for four cars. Some old mine buildings are located here. A little road drops down to the right and terminates in a good picnic spot a hundred yards down, beside the La Plata River.

The hike starts with its first hazard—crossing the river. Since this area has a good deal of foot traffic, there is usually a pretty good log to cross over. Just over the river two or three hundred yards you come to the ruins of the Gold King Mill. It was one of the largest ever to operate in the canyon. It can be seen easily from the west side of the river and is another sign that you are at the right place. It is still impressive even in its state of decay. Much of the roof structure remains intact. It was

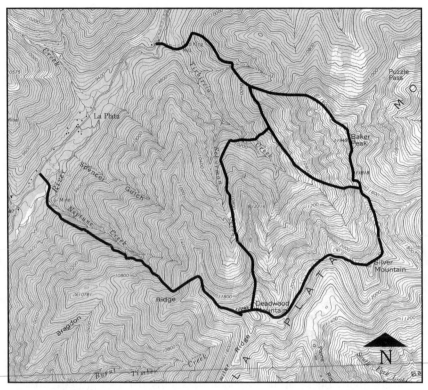

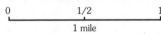

Silver Mountain

a large stamping operation that continued well into the twentieth century.

The hike basically follows Tirbircio Creek up to its headwaters in the basin on the west side of the peak of Silver Mountain.
However, the first half of the creek is in a sharp canyon most of
the time. So from the Gold King Mill, hike north up an old road;
it soon swings east and follows the creek (east-southeast) but
remains high above it. The road quits at an old mine after a mile
and a quarter of steady climbing. Bushwhacking is required from
this point, but it is not too difficult because you continue in the
same basic direction. Silver Mountain is visible straight ahead
most of the time. Before too long, you will emerge above timberline and have mostly talus the rest of the way.

As you work your way (in the same direction) up into the
basin, turn left and climb 700 feet to a saddle between Silver
Mountain and Baker Peak, which lies one mile northwest of
Silver. It is lower at 11,949 feet. The climb up the saddle is steep
and slow, but after that it is fairly easy to the top. Turn right at
the saddle and hike one-half mile southeast to the summit, which
is another 750 feet higher.

From the top, you look eastward, down into the headwaters
of Lightner Creek, and much farther beyond, Durango appears
safely tucked into the Animas Valley. To the north and west are
the many peaks of the La Plata Mountains. To the northeast on
the distant skyline is Mountain View Crest and, just beyond, the
Needles, with three peaks above 14,000 feet. To the south is
New Mexico. The top of Silver Mountain is a nice smooth roll
where you can be comfortable taking leisurely views if there is
no wind.

The 5.3-mile round trip assumes return by the approach
route, but there are two other alternatives. One is Baker Peak.
To do this, start back the way you came; at the saddle, continue
northwest to the top of Baker in another quarter-mile. There is
an intermediate point of 150 feet to climb and descend before
reaching Baker. From the top of Baker you get a fine view north
to the next La Plata peak, Lewis Mountain. It is rocky and rough.

To descend from Baker, continue northwest along the ridge
one-half mile to the beginning of timberline, then swing west
down toward Tirbircio Creek. There is no trail in this area,
but you should reach the old road that you ascended in about

Silver Mountain. Mount Baker is on the left ridge; Deadwood Mountain and its descending ridge are on the right.

three-quarters of a mile. From there on, it is simply a matter of following the road back to Gold King Mill.

Another alternate return from Silver is over Deadwood Mountain. It lies southwest of Silver via a connecting ridge just over a mile long. However, since the ridge is similar to an S-curve, start hiking off Silver northwest a quarter-mile, then southwest a half-mile, and finally west a quarter-mile to the top of Deadwood at 12,285 feet. To come off Deadwood, go straight north down a ridge or back east a couple of hundred yards to a little saddle and then north down a couloir into a small branch of Tirbircio Creek. Either route has some steep terrain near the top. In the couloir, a small branch of Tirbircio Creek starts; it will lead you back to the main creek in a mile. Those starting down the ridge can swing a little to the right after a half-mile and join this branch or follow the ridge down about a mile and then swing to the right to Tirbircio itself. Most of this descent will be in the timber. Going all the way to the end of the ridge is apt to put you above some cliffs. Follow the creek down to the starting point.

An easier way off Deadwood takes you straight west to the river; its disadvantage is a harder river crossing (though sometimes

there are logs over it), and it leaves you a mile to hike back
upstream on the main road to your car. To take this route, hike
the west ridge of Deadwood; after a few hundred yards it starts to
descend. There is a kind of trail along here that can be helpful; a
part of the time the trail is quite good. After the descent begins it
gets quite steep in places, but soon comes to a mining road. This
descends all the way to the river following along the south side of
Neptune Creek, which is visible only occasionally. After crossing
the river, you should find a little road leading west up to the
main road, where you will need to turn right to return to your
parking place.

Tomahawk Basin–Diorite Peak

Distance: *2 miles (round trip)*
Starting elevation: *10,900 feet*
Elevation gain: *1,861 feet*
High point: *12,761 feet*
Rating: *Moderate to hard*
Time allowed: *2.5 to 3.5 hours*
Maps: *7.5'La Plata; San Juan National Forest*

This is another hike out of La Plata Canyon. It should not be
attempted earlier than late July (except in years when the snowpack is below average) because of an avalanche path that usually
fills La Plata Canyon Road not far above Lewis Creek. It takes a
long time for the snow to melt and the forest service does not
plow the road, but mining companies sometimes do.

To make this climb, take La Plata Canyon Road three miles
north of Kroeger Campground, where there is a small parking
area. The Gold King Mill is just across the river to the east. The
road beyond this spot is rough, but two-wheel-drives can usually
make it one and three-quarters miles up the road to the
Tomahawk Basin turnoff.

The Tomahawk turnoff is sharply uphill to the left. The
canyon road itself is narrow here. Two-wheel-drives will need to

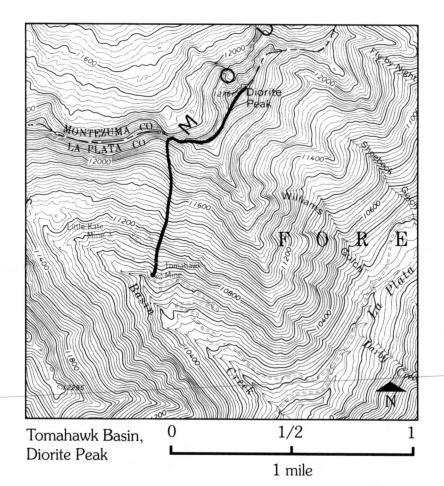

Tomahawk Basin,
Diorite Peak

0   1/2   1

1 mile

park a little before or a little beyond the turnoff. Tomahawk Basin Road is very rough, steep, and narrow—two-wheel-drives should not attempt this road at all. Parking at the turnoff will add 1.6 miles (one way) and 1,000 feet of climb to the hike. Four-wheel-drives can go up this 1.6 miles and park out of the way at the Tomahawk Mine.

The hike is without benefit of trail but is easy to follow because it quickly gets above timberline, where everything is visible. Above timberline, most of the hike is on loose talus rock.

Begin hiking north up the mountainside toward the low spot in the saddle. There will be a ridge running southeast on your right. A few hundred feet below the saddle is the site of an airplane crash from the early 1960s. This was a military flight in which two men were killed. The tragedy was all the more ironic since 300 feet more of altitude would have allowed them to clear the ridge. The crash and many snows have scattered the wreckage over a wide area. Most of it has been salvaged, but climbers will no doubt see some scraps of aluminum skin, wires, and other smaller parts as they climb through the area.

Once at the saddle, turn right, climb to the high point of the ridge, and follow it around northeast to Diorite. This is a half-mile from the saddle.

The views from the top are breathtaking. Immediately below, steeply down on the west side, you look into Bear Creek Basin. This is wild country, not visited by many humans. On the far side of the basin are Mount Moss and Centennial Peak (formerly Banded Mountain). The connecting ridge between them is extremely rough and forbidding. Across this ridge and a little beyond is Hesperus Peak, at 13,232 feet the highest point in the La Platas. North of Centennial, Sharkstooth rises steeply to a sharp point. To the north there is a complete panorama of peaks, including, from west to east, the San Miguels with their three fourteeners and the distinctive Lizard Head shaft, Grizzly Peak, Engineer Mountain, the Twilights, the Needles, and many more. To the east, near at hand, are La Plata Canyon and the east ridge of the La Plata Mountains.

Hikers should return by the same route they ascended.

The route can be made a little easier but slightly longer by driving another quarter-mile beyond the Tomahawk Mine to the Little Kate Mine, where there is generous parking space. At this point begin hiking up and right on what appears at first to be a drivable road, but that soon ceases to be so. This route zigzags upward a half-mile and stops at an upper mine. From here a trail goes on up toward the saddle on the ridge, zigzagging on the way. The trail stops below the ridge, but a short scramble completes that part. Once on the ridge, turn right and follow on up to the false summit and beyond a short distance to the top of Diorite. This route reduces the altitude to be gained through hiking by 200 feet.

Centennial Peak and Sharkstooth

Distance: 4.4 miles (add .5 mile for Sharkstooth) (round trip)
Starting elevation: 10,900 feet
Elevation gain: 2,162 feet (plus 526 feet for Sharkstooth)
High point: 13,062 feet
Rating: Centennial—moderate; Sharkstooth—hard
Time allowed: 3 hours to Centennial and back (from Durango this is an all-day trip because of the long drive)
Maps: 7.5'La Plata; San Juan National Forest

This hike is described as a climb to the top of Centennial Peak with an optional side trip to the top of Sharkstooth.

A fairly long drive is involved; the last eight miles of it are through tall aspen forest with occasional breaks in the trees to reveal the western profile of the La Platas. These are the highest peaks in the range but are not often seen because lower peaks block the view from all directions except west. This territory is unpopulated for a number of miles. As you approach from the west, the glimpses that you get are of Hesperus (at 13,232 feet the highest peak in the La Platas), Moss, Spiller, Centennial, and Sharkstooth; all except Sharkstooth are over 13,000 feet. Although a bit shorter, Sharkstooth captures your attention because of its sharp triangular shape thrusting abruptly into the sky above the pass. From this angle it definitely looks like a shark's tooth.

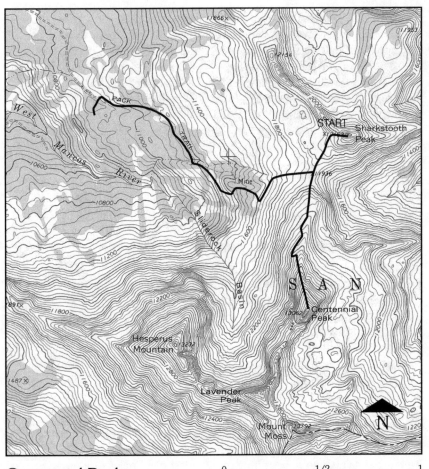

Centennial Peak
and Sharkstooth

To take this hike, go north out of Mancos on the Dolores road, State Highway 184. Just a quarter-mile north of Mancos, turn right uphill on the road marked for Jackson Reservoir and Transfer Campground. After it enters the national forest, this road is labeled #561 and is a good gravel road. Follow it a total of twelve miles from Mancos to a point two miles beyond Transfer Park where #350 (Spruce Mill Road) joins it. Road 561 goes north here; take 350 east. It is still a good gravel road, though narrow and winding at times. At about six and one-half miles a small road, labeled "Twin Lakes, Sharkstooth Trail," drops off to the right. This road takes you one and one-half miles, past Twin Lakes, to the trailhead, where it stops. This road is rough, and rocky in places; when it is dry, ordinary cars can make it with a little care. At the trailhead the road turns sharply right, and there is room here to park several cars.

The trail begins in big spruce and fir and moves steadily uphill to the saddle between Sharkstooth and Centennial. This is an easy and well-defined trail. Part way up is an old mine on the left. Near this same area, at the south end of a switchback, is a breathtaking view of Hesperus Peak on the right and Centennial on the left. A very jagged ridge and Lavender Peak are in between.

Centennial is a bit shorter than Hesperus and is distinguished from the sharper peaks by a roll top. Both Centennial and Hesperus are characterized by bands of different-colored sedimentary rocks. In fact, Centennial was called Banded Mountain until its name was officially changed July 30, 1976, in celebration of the Colorado state centennial. This was, of course, the same month in which the United States was celebrating its bicentennial. This mountain is listed on the La Plata quad map as Banded Mountain.

At the saddle, turn south (right) off the trail, which at that point goes east and drops deeply into Bear Creek Canyon. When you turn right, there is no more trail to follow, but you cannot get lost—just climb upward seven-tenths of a mile to the summit. You start up steeply over talus; after 150 yards you come to a much more gradual slope over tundra. Stay near the high point of the ridge. As you get near the top, it will be rocky again. There are some paths showing in this area.

Each time I have climbed this mountain there has been a strong, cold west wind; it seems to be a regular pattern for the

Climbing Centennial from the saddle on the trail, with Sharkstooth in the background.

area. Be sure to have warm clothes along, including gloves, even in the summer. My first climb of Centennial was during the last week of December. There was not much snow that year, only four to six inches on the exposed parts of the mountain and less below. But even though it was a beautiful sunny day, the members of our group nearly froze because of the bitterly cold wind. Fortunately, at the top we only had to take a few steps down to a ledge on the east side to complete shelter from the wind. Here we ate lunch and viewed the scenery in comfort. One of the first men to the top had thoughtfully brought along his little propane pack stove and had hot bouillon ready to serve the freezing later arrivals—just the right thing at the right time and place.

The views from the top are excellent in all directions except south, where the neighboring peaks are the whole view. To the southeast toward Durango you cannot quite see the city, but you can see Fort Lewis College, which is located on a mesa 300 feet above Durango on its east side. To the north you can see the full sweep of the San Juans, from the Needles northeast to the San Miguels northwest. Even farther west are the Blues in Utah, and to the southwest the Sleeping Ute.

The return trip should be made to the saddle and back down the trail you ascended.

The climb up Centennial Peak is not really difficult, but talus and the altitude make it deserve a moderate rating.

If you wish to climb Sharkstooth on this same excursion, simply attack its south side from the saddle. It is only 526 feet above the saddle, but it is much more difficult than Centennial. It starts over ordinary talus but gets steeper and steeper as you rise. There are plenty of rocks to grab, but the trouble is that most of them are loose, and it is very easy to start a rock slide. No member of a climbing party should be immediately below another. Near the top, every handhold and foothold must be tested for solidity before trusting your weight to it.

The top is very small, and the north face drops even more precipitously than the south face. The views are much the same as from Centennial. The descent must be done with even more care than the ascent because of the longer reach of the legs and the loose rocks.

This climb is short and quick. (I made it to the top in twenty minutes from the saddle.) But it must be rated hard because of the loose-rock hazard.

Hesperus Mountain

Distance: *5 miles (round trip)*
Starting elevation: *10,900 feet*
Elevation gain: *2,332 feet*
High point: *13,232 feet*
Rating: *Difficult*
Time allowed: *4 to 6 hours*
Maps: *7.5' La Plata; San Juan National Forest*

Hesperus Peak is the highest point in the La Plata Mountains. It makes a good one-day hike and climb; its summit gives almost a complete 360-degree view. To the south and southeast, nearby peaks cut off some valley views. Hesperus is a

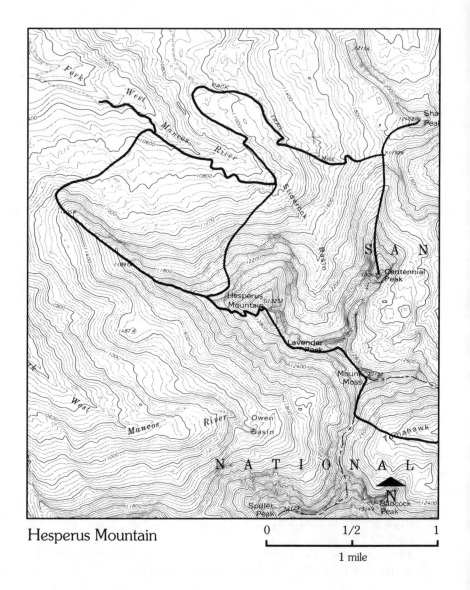

Hesperus Mountain

0   1/2   1

1 mile

handsome mountain and well worth the climb. It is not seen very often except at considerable distance, and this is mainly from the west. The eastern and southern parts of the La Platas and other San Juan peaks cut off views of it from the populated areas and highways.

The peak is to be climbed from the west ridge. This can be done from the north or the south side of the ridge. The south side is approached via the Echo Basin road two miles east of Mancos. The more usual route is by the north side of the ridge; this route is described here.

You used to be able to go north of Mancos to Transfer Park and then east for this climb, but a landslide has closed off the road two miles in from the park. Now the best route for a north-side approach to the mountain is to go into the Sharkstooth trailhead. This access is described in the previous hike, "Centennial Peak and Sharkstooth," so it will not be repeated here. At this trailhead a new trail was constructed in 1990, called "West Mancos Trail No. 621." Take it south toward Hesperus Mountain, now quite visible and dominating the southern view above the forest. The trail starts on an old road but soon becomes a very good trail through the woods. From the point of view of the Hesperus climber, two unfortunate things happen: the trail swings east for some distance and then begins to lose altitude. This is necessary to cross the North Fork of the West Mancos River up near its headwaters; it is crossed in three-quarters of a mile over a good log bridge. Then the trail immediately swings west and stays near the river but continues to descend fairly rapidly. Shortly after crossing the stream and before renewing its descent, the trail comes into a clearing where the north face of Hesperus, beginning almost at your feet, confronts you in all its massive grandeur. When I was there in mid-October it was largely covered with new snow when everything lower was bare, thus adding even more to its impressiveness.

At this point, experienced climbers looking for a challenge may want to try the short but more difficult route and start the ascent immediately. It saves considerable distance over the easier route described below. You can work out your own approach, but it is better to move up southwest on a course that is less steep and later more directly south toward the top of the main west ridge. This ridge ascends gradually up to a point where the

Hesperus Mountain from the western-approach road: Centennial Peak is off its left shoulder and Sharkstooth is at the far left.

predominate gray of the rocks turns to a dark red and an abruptly steeper grade. If you can strike the top of the ridge here, you will find a trail coming up along the crest of the ridge. Follow it on to the summit.

For climbers of more modest accomplishments it is best to go much farther west and start up the west ridge of the peak where it has descended to a lower level. Unfortunately, this presents a dilemma, for the trail continues to descend fairly rapidly. Your choice starts where you are standing at 10,800 feet with a little over 2,400 feet to go to the top. One choice is to abandon the trail, climbing up toward the face to near tree line and then west for most of a mile, largely on talus rock. This will take you to a point where the ridge can be climbed at a much lower and easier level. This route is nearly level, but talus, though not difficult, is much slower than trail. The other option is to follow the trail down another mile and a quarter to an old timber cut. Here the trail joins an abandoned logging road. (The main problem with this route is that by this time you have descended another 400 feet.) Anywhere within the next couple hundred yards you should leave the trail and start uphill, finding your own route

Glissading off Hesperus.

through the band of big timber, which is several hundred yards wide at this point. You should emerge into the same talus area after twenty to thirty minutes. Here choose a route of ascent toward the lower end of the west ridge. Once on top of the ridge you should find a route worn into a trail, heading left for the summit. It is easy for three-quarters of a mile, up to 12,400 feet. At this point you are confronted with a steep rise through a red formation. The last 800 feet will be steeper and rocky but not particularly difficult, so take heart. There is a good trail up this steep rise on the left side; then the trail crosses over to the right side and stays there the rest of the way to the top. Part of the time you will be on loose rock, part of the time on ledge. The small rocks here have a nice clinking sound, thus playing music for you as you climb.

The summit is not large but is enough of a roll to support several people comfortably as they eat their well-earned sandwiches and absorb the great panorama. There are connecting ridges to Mount Lavender and Mount Moss southeast and to Centennial northeast via Lavender. The one to Centennial looks impossible to cross, but I have a technical-climbing friend who told

me he had done it. I did the route via Mount Moss in the summer
of 1990 with a friend. It starts from Tomahawk Basin off the west
side of La Plata Canyon, climbing to the head of the Basin then
across Moss and Lavender to Hesperus. This is a much more difficult route; we were able to do it in a day. By the rating scheme
used in this book I would call it very hard. Moss and Lavender are
not too bad until the last pitch on Lavender, which is close to
straight up but possible because of the broken character of the
rock. It gives rewarding views. From Lavender across to Hesperus
is difficult and a bit discouraging due to several gashes in low
points, some of them difficult though not technical.

The return trip for the main route described here is the same
as the approach, back down the west ridge. However, a little way
to the west of the red ledge there is, in the early summer, a
snowy chute that can provide a good glissade for those equipped
with ice axes and proper experience. The top is quite steep and
can be hazardous for the novice. It does offer a quick and excit-
ing way down the steep part of the ridge.

Because of the talus, the steepness, and the total altitude
gain, this hike is rated difficult. However, most anyone in good
health and with patience and some carefulness should be able to
make it and enjoy it.

Parrott Peak

Distance: *6 miles (round trip)*
Starting elevation: *8,600 feet*
Elevation gain: *3,257 feet*
High point: *11,857 feet*
Rating: *Moderate*
Time allowed: *5 hours*
Maps: *7.5'Hesperus; 7.5'La Plata; San Juan National Forest*

This is an interesting climb in the fall, when higher areas are
snowed in. It has the advantage of a southern exposure, which
keeps the snow off later in the fall and takes it off earlier in the

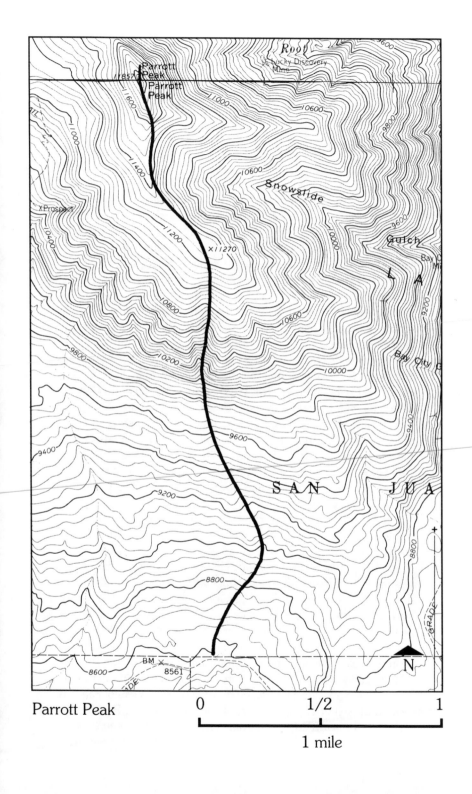

Parrott Peak

spring. It is also quickly accessible from Durango. The described route requires a four-wheel-drive to get to the starting point, but this only involves an extra two miles (each way) for those with two-wheel-drive transportation. This would also add an extra 440 feet of altitude gain.

To reach this area, drive west of Durango on Highway 160 5.6 miles west of Hesperus to the Cherry Creek National Forest picnic area. Just beyond this a little four-wheel-drive road turns north uphill through a gate (which is normally either open or not locked). Two-wheel-drive vehicles can make it part way up this road when it is dry, but it climbs steeply in places and has a couple of very rough spots. At one mile this road reaches an old railroad right-of-way. Turn right and follow this east one and one-half miles. There is a side route here that will allow you to drive a short distance uphill, where you can park in a clearing near the timber.

The hike is basically bushwhacking, although there are some trails from time to time that can be followed profitably. They are not official national forest trails and are not maintained. They're just paths maintained by traffic, both bovine and human.

An interesting feature that you may want to hike around lies just east along the railroad right-of-way. It is a large landslide area involving many acres. It is not in the steep area but the flatter level below the steep part. It is a very chewed-up piece of land with lots of cracks and ups and downs. The right-of-way is dislocated, so that you cannot drive on it any farther.

For the climb, head north through the timber. After a mile and a quarter the going gets quite steep. This lasts a little over one-half mile and brings you to the top of a partially cleared ridge. The actual top is another mile northwest along this ridge, most of it easy hiking. The top is above timberline and affords fine views down into La Plata Canyon and across the canyon to the eastern range of the La Plata peaks. There are also good views south to the mesa country and on into New Mexico.

The return trip should follow the same general route as the approach. There is nothing really difficult on this trip, but the total altitude gain is substantial; therefore, the trip is rated moderate.

There is an alternate route you may want to consider that is easier and also offers the option of climbing Madden Peak and Parrott in the same trip. This route shows on the San Juan

National Forest map but better on the topo maps; it lies princi-
pally on the 7.5′Thompson Peak Quad topo. To take this route,
drive to the top of Mancos Hill on Highway 160, just over
halfway from Hesperus to the town of Mancos. At the top of the
hill turn north on a gravel road into a fairly flat area; after a mile
this road curves to the right and starts ascending. In another half-
mile the road splits; here take the left turn (the better road). The
road goes on approximately another three miles, passing prominent radio towers a short distance to the left on a separate road.
At this point the gravel stops at a cattleguard, but the road goes
on. In wet weather two-wheel-drive vehicles may find it advisable
to stop here. Others can go on most of another mile and park in
a big meadow. Hiking should start by going on up this same road
another half-mile to another split in the road. Either branch of it
can be taken from here. The left fork takes you to the top of a
ridge where you should turn right off the road and follow the
ridge directly to the summit of Madden Peak (11,972 feet), in
about a mile. There is a trail along much of this ridge; it is an
easy climb. To do Parrott from there go down a ridge to the right
(about ninety degrees from the ascent ridge). This is a little east
of straight south. Here you drop down to a saddle at 11,560 feet
before ascending another 300 feet to the top of Parrott. If you
choose the right fork of the road at the split you will stay in a
basin below the Madden ridge and head straight for the saddle;
this is mostly east with a little bias to the north. It is basically easy
going. At the saddle you have a choice as to which peak to do
first. Madden is to the left, Parrott to the right. You can easily do
either one or both.

Madden Peak, Parrott, Star

Distance: *7 to 10 miles (depending on peaks climbed)*
Starting elevation: *9,000 feet*
Elevation gain: *2,972 feet (top of Madden)*
High point: *11,972 feet*
Rating: *Moderate to hard*
Time allowed: *4 hours (for only one peak)*
Maps: *7.5' Hesperus; 7.5' La Plata; San Juan National Forest*

Parrott Peak with an optional route to Madden was just described. This hike, with Madden as the starting destination, is from a totally different route. The previous account is from the south with an option from the west. This account is from the east side out of La Plata Canyon; the scenery and perspective are totally different until you reach the top. During the ascent there are great views from time to time into the canyon and across it to the eastern ridge of La Plata Peaks. Much of the time at first you are in the seclusion of deep timber.

For this ascent take the La Plata Canyon road one-third mile west of Hesperus; it goes north off U.S. Highway 160. After going through the village of Mayday it enters the canyon. After passing the Kroeger National Forest Campground on the left and a little farther on a private picnic ground operated by one of the lodge fraternities, you come in 300 yards to a little mining road that turns left uphill off the main road. Take this road. It is six and three-quarters miles from U.S. 160; there is an old green bus set up in the edge of the woods here for use as a cabin. This is basically a four-wheel-drive road, although you might try the first pitch with your two-wheel-drive; if you make it to the first switchback, you probably can make the rest of the road. Distances given in the heading assume you will be hiking all of this road. Just around that switchback there is a wire gate that may be closed. If it is and you go through, be sure to close it after you because there likely are cows grazing above. Drive on from here

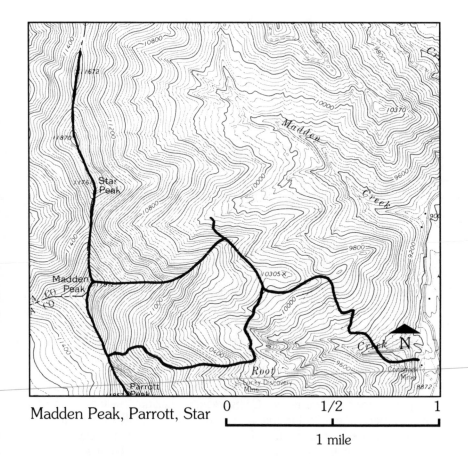

Madden Peak, Parrott, Star

| 0 | 1/2 | 1 |

1 mile

to a point where the road splits at one and one-half miles above the main road.

For the climb, either direction will do. The left route has about 300 feet less climbing, but it is steeper and harder, though shorter. It swings south and then west, then south again. At the last swing south you should park out of the way and start climbing. Driving any farther south brings you on to a private mining claim, one that has been worked recently. At the bend in the road you can see a steep, open grassy area leading west up to a saddle on the main ridge at the foot of Parrott Peak on the south and Madden on the north. There is no trail here, but you should be able to make this all right. The grass and other vegetation is quite tall later in the summer, and if it's wet it can soak your legs quickly. You may want to wear gaiters or rain pants. At the ridge, Parrott comes down in a cliff; just around the end on the west side it can be climbed. It is very steep at first but soon improves. The summit, at 11,857 feet, can be reached in a few hundred yards; it is only about 340 feet above the saddle level. Madden is to the right of the saddle, a quarter-mile to the top, and easier to climb, up a good walk-up slope. Its height is 11,972 feet, a gain of 447 feet from the saddle. If you are still ambitious you may want to go on to Star Peak, one-third mile farther north on the ridge. It is 11,761 feet, with a rise of 321 feet from the saddle between it and Madden. There are three more unnamed ridge points north of Star before Gibbs Peak, and all are easily climbed.

Back at the split in the approach road, the route to the right goes north. In three-tenths of a mile it crosses a little flat place where the main canyon is on the right below, but there is a small drop on the left side to what appears to be a good camping site. Park here out of the way. Just beyond this spot the road divides, the main route starting downhill; take the smaller one, which bears left and up a grade. At about a hundred yards you reach the crest of a ridge that is descending from the west. Take this ridge in a sharp left turn and follow it all the way to the top of Madden Peak, about a mile of distance and an elevation gain of just over 2,000 feet. Most of it isn't bad hiking, but there are a few steep spots. There is a recognizable trail along much of this way, apparently used by cows and horseback riders. It is worth following much of the time, but don't worry if you don't find it or lose it. Just stay near the point of the ridge and keep going up; it goes directly to the summit. At the top, Parrott will be to the left (south) and Star and the unnamed points to the right (north).

You might want to make this a loop hike, going up one of these routes and down the other. From the top of Madden to the saddle between it and Parrott is the upper-level distance between the two routes, about one-quarter mile.

Another interesting option would be to go to the top of the ridge by one of these routes and then north along the ridge to climb all of its summits to and including Gibbs, coming down from Gibbs. To go any farther north involves different problems and a return to this point, or a much longer drive and far more difficult climbing if you want to go on as far as Burwell and Spiller. You can leave a spare car on the Gibbs approach route; for this, see the description for Gibbs Peak, below. This adds some to the altitude gained because Gibbs's summit is at 12,286 feet, but it does not add much to the mileage because the parking spot here is much higher than the starting point.

Gibbs Peak

Distance: *2 miles (round trip)*
Starting elevation: *10,850 feet*
Elevation gain: *1,436 feet*
High point: *12,286 feet*
Rating: *Moderate*
Time allowed: *1.5 to 2 hours*
Maps: *7.5'La Plata; San Juan National Forest*

Gibbs Peak is in the La Plata Mountains northwest of Durango. From the top of the four-wheel-drive road to the summit involves only about one mile of climbing. As high peaks go, it is fairly easy, but it is rated moderate because much of the hike requires steep walking.

The approach is made via La Plata Canyon, a beautiful drive in itself. To get there, take U.S. Highway 160 west out of Durango eleven miles. One-third mile beyond the Hesperus

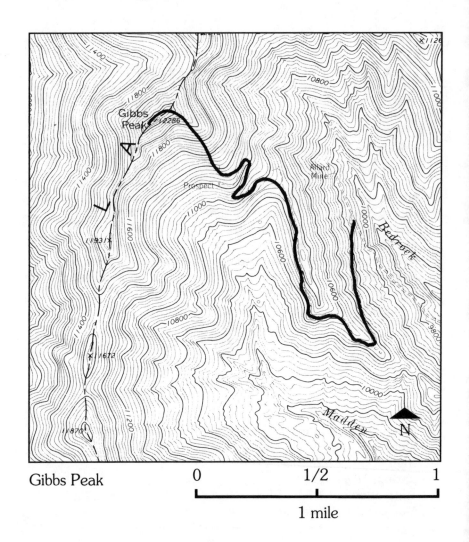

Gibbs Peak

turnoff, take a right turn (north). This road starts off as blacktop; in four miles, just beyond the mining town of Mayday, it becomes gravel and enters La Plata Canyon, following along the west side of the La Plata River. Two miles farther is Kroeger Campground. This is a lovely place to camp if you are so minded. It is set in the flat among big trees with easy access to the river; it is a good launching place for hiking, jeeping, fishing, and picnicking. Kroeger is a forest service campground. The whole canyon is a popular place in the summer, with rugged high peaks on each side, lingering snow until July, many high waterfalls, big spruce, fir and aspen trees, and some of the most prolific wildflowers to be found anywhere.

For the Gibbs Peak climb, go another mile and a half beyond Kroeger Campground and turn left uphill on a little side road just before crossing Bedrock Creek. Two-wheel-drive cars should park one and one-half miles up this road where the road goes straight on to the Allard Mine. At this point, four-wheel-drives should make a sharp left turn and go on up the hill. (Those who must start hiking here should follow the same road. It adds 1.4 miles and 750 feet of altitude.) The parking place for four-wheel-drives is at the end of a half-mile straight stretch in the road, just below the top of a ridge. The road switches back left at this point. It is possible to drive a bit higher, but parking is less generous.

Begin hiking on up the road. It makes a couple of switchbacks and soon runs into trees down across the road. It is possible to follow the road farther around and up the hillside, but it is shorter just to start climbing west up the mountainside toward the top. There is no trail, but you should not get lost as long as you are going up. The forest here is not very cluttered with brush and downed timber. In a few hundred yards you emerge above timberline and climb on loose rocks most of the rest of the way. Just before the top there is a short distance of scrambling over firm rocky ledges where there is some exposure. Once over this, you just follow the roll top southwest to the highest point.

The west ridge of the La Platas is a bit higher than the east ridge. Gibbs Peak is about 1,000 feet lower than the highest of the west ridge peaks, but it affords fine views to the south, where nothing is higher. In this direction, you can see all the way into New Mexico and Arizona. Seventy-five miles south and a little west is Shiprock, a distinctive stone shaft pointing skyward. It is an ancient volcanic plug that thrusts 1,800 feet above its surrounding terrain. It is a sacred place to the Navajos. This should be quite visible from Gibbs except on very hazy or cloudy days.

Eastward from Gibbs you get a complete survey of La Plata Canyon and the east range of the La Plata Mountains; it is rugged and beautiful country. Westward is the East Mancos River valley, and beyond lie the towns of Mancos and Cortez. In the distance and a bit north are the Blue and La Sal mountains near Monticello and Moab, Utah. To the north, and near at hand, are the highest peaks of the La Platas.

The hike planned here returns by the approach route. However, ambitious hikers with plenty of time may want to add the challenge of Burwell Peak. At 12,664 feet it is 378 feet higher than Gibbs. Those who try this should exercise due care, for there are some rough spots in the mile of ridge that leads northeast from Gibbs to Burwell, including some precipitous drops off the east side. Another half-mile beyond Burwell lies Spiller Peak at 13,123 feet, one of five La Plata peaks that rise above 13,000 feet. Babcock, another thirteener, is next in line, but it should not be approached from this side.

Hikes between Durango and Silverton

Hermosa Trail

Distance: *8 miles (round trip), with additional options*
Starting elevation: *7,800 feet*
Elevation gain: *200 feet*
High point: *8,000 feet*
Rating: *Easy*
Time allowed: *3.5 to 4.5 hours*
Maps: *7.5'Hermosa; 7.5'Monument Hill; 7.5'Elk Creek; San Juan National Forest*

Hermosa Trail is in the heart of a very large roadless area. There are high ridges and many canyons. The whole area contains many thousands of acres. The main trail is sixteen miles long, and there are many side trails. To explore this area thoroughly would take many days of backpacking. However, good day and half-day hikes can be done from both the south and north ends quite easily.

This is excellent elk-hunting territory and has good trout streams as well. There are also many deer.

The trail at first follows the contour of Hermosa Creek but is several hundred feet above it so that you look down into the canyon below and up at the heavily wooded mountains. Across the canyon, the hills rise up above timberline to the 13,000-foot peaks of the La Platas.

The trail is one of the widest, best maintained, and most heavily used in southwestern Colorado. It is also one of the easiest to hike, for there is no major altitude change. Along the trail are big trees, open vistas, and wildflowers.

To get to the trail, take U.S. Highway 550 ten miles north of Durango to Hermosa Village. Just north of the bridge over Hermosa Creek, and before the railroad crossing, turn left on a

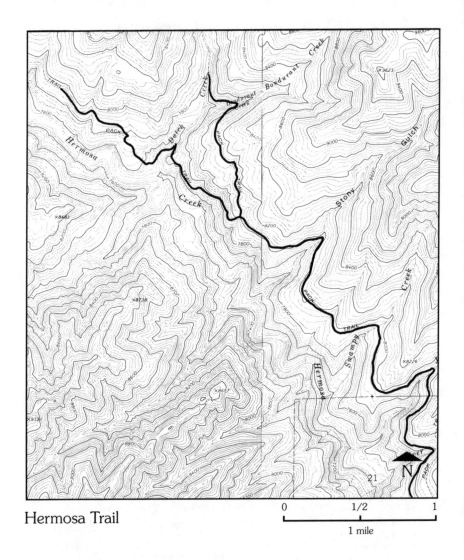

Hermosa Trail

little side road. In a distance of just several yards, this road meets a north-south road that parallels the highway. Turn right (north) here, and follow this road uphill to its end in four miles. The first half or more of it is blacktop and the rest gravel. At the dead end, park off to the side and begin the hike just off the end of the road. The trail goes sharply down for about twenty yards, then meets the main trail, which you should take to the right. This point should be carefully studied and remembered for the sake of the return trip, because it is easy to miss this "exit ramp." A miss takes you not only past your car, but quickly onto private property.

The main trail crosses several side streams that may be fairly well dried up or they may be flowing and muddy, making hiking boots useful though not needed on other parts of the trail.

At four miles, the trail divides. This is where the options begin. The left branch descends 500 feet in the next mile to a good footbridge across Dutch Creek. Just beyond here, you can step off to the left to Hermosa Creek itself. Both of these are good fishing streams. Hiking beyond this brings you back up to the previous level. You can continue on as far as interest and time permit.

If you take the right branch at the trail split, you are on the Dutch Creek Trail, though you do not see the creek itself until you go up the trail a mile. There is one fairly steep hill of about 250 feet that you go down before reaching the creek. Again, you can hike on this trail as far as time and interest permit. There is a small open grassy meadow where you first come to the stream.

Whichever trail you take, return by the same route to the road and your parking place.

Those who may want to consider doing the entire length of the trail have two options. One is to backpack, spending at least one night on the trail; the other is to spend a long day hiking at a good pace with only a few short rest periods. This is best done from the north end because there is a net drop of 1,000 feet from north to south. It is not all downhill, however; there is the 500-foot climb out of the Dutch Creek Valley described above plus two other rather large hills. It is a very rewarding hike, with ever-changing scenery, starting out in a wide meadow bounded by forest on the mounting sides of the valley and followed by low canyon walls, ending as a traverse of the mountainside with the

Hiking on the Hermosa Trail.

creek far below and the top high above. The scenery is spectacular, especially during the fall color season, from the last week of September through the first ten days of October. Most of the time the trail is very clear, but there are a few grassy spots where it may be difficult to follow; when I did the full length the most obscure spot was a few miles in from the north end at the site of an old cabin. There is a trail crossing Hermosa Creek at this point. I picked it up and followed it a little way before deciding it couldn't be right; crossing back I soon picked up the right trail again south of the cabin and had no more problems following it after that.

For access to the north end see the following hike description for Corral Draw–Hermosa Trail.

All of this area is excellent for elk. An especially good place to look for them is in the aspen trees at the beginning of Dutch Creek Trail.

Corral Draw–Hermosa Trail

Distance: 10 miles (one way)
Starting elevation: 10,900 feet
Elevation loss: 2,400 feet (300 feet regained)
Low point: 8,500 feet
Rating: Moderate
Time allowed: 5 to 6 hours
Maps: 7.5′ Elk Creek; 7.5′ Hermosa Peak; San Juan National Forest

This is a partial loop or point-to-point hike. The Corral Draw Trail was rebuilt in 1990 and now makes a good hike combined with the northern end of Hermosa Trail. I am describing it as starting at the top and descending to Hermosa with a gentle climb out to the Hermosa trailhead. Of course, it could be hiked the other way, but Corral Draw is a substantial climb. It stays near the drainage except near the top and is mostly in heavy timber. The part of the Hermosa Trail used here starts out in a

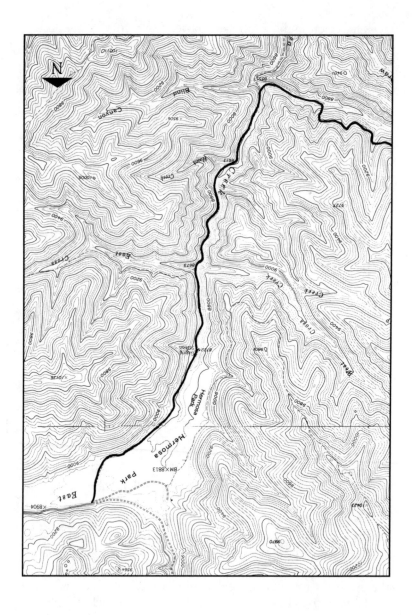

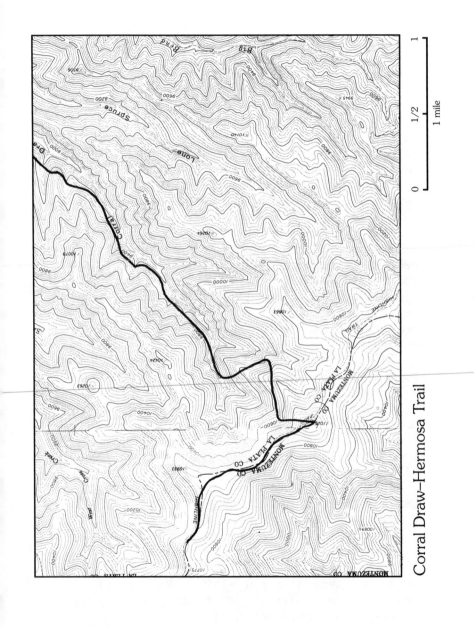

Corral Draw–Hermosa Trail

0   1/2   1

1 mile

canyon with timber above and then moves out into a wider graceful meadow at the upper end.

This pair of trails is northwest of Purgatory Ski Area, which is located just off U.S. 550 twenty-eight miles north of Durango. Take the Purgatory road west off the highway to the northeast corner of the large parking lot. Here pick up the gravel road (Forest Service 578) going north; it soon turns back west and climbs in several switchbacks up the ski hill, with some of the runs visible to the south. At the top, the road turns north; in a half-mile it turns left downhill off the road that continues on north. Your road goes west down into Hermosa Park, a nice secluded meadowed valley. In about five miles, where the road is down at the bottom of the valley, there is a little road that turns off left (south) and soon fords the East Fork of Hermosa Creek, usually a small stream. Just beyond the stream there is a nice trailhead area with generous parking, a corral, and toilet facilities. Park your extra car here.

Take the other car back to the main road and continue west on it. The gravel stops at this point, and the road goes on the rest of the way over dirt; the steep parts can be difficult when they are wet.

The road swings northwest and in a little over a mile it fords the main stream of Hermosa Creek. This is a wide crossing with a rocky bottom. After the spring snowmelt (the third week of June or later in some years) most cars can make this if the driver does not slow down enough to lose momentum through the water. Four-wheel-drives are better here, but except for this problem other cars should have no difficulty with any of the road when it is dry.

About a mile beyond the ford turn sharply left on the Hotel Draw road (FS 550). Follow it through a valley and to the top of the ridge in three and one-half miles. Continue following the road, now going south along the ridge, to a split. The right side (550) goes down the west side of the ridge via Scotch Creek to the Dolores Valley. The left side (now FS 564) is your road; follow it a little over a hundred yards to the Colorado Trail. Park here and take the trail south, at first steeply uphill, for a mile to where the Corral Draw Trail starts off left.

Hikers who want to approach this trail from the west side should take the Roaring Forks Road east off State Highway 145, some seven miles south of Rico. It starts out as Forest Service 435; later it meets 564—take this left. In several more miles it meets the Colorado Trail a mile and one-half north of Orphan Butte. Stay with the road another four to five miles, where it should meet the Colorado Trail again. (They have been paralleling each other for these miles.) Here you can park and hike the Colorado Trail northeast about a mile to the Corral Draw trailhead, which will now be a right turn. The road at the junction with the trail swings off left and away from the trail for two miles or a little more.

Corral Draw now descends 2,400 feet in five and one-half miles in a well-defined trail, much of the time through a meadow but sometimes in large timber. Hunters like this trail in the fall.

At the bottom of the route, Hermosa Creek must be crossed. It is a large stream and may have to be waded. The crossing has recently been moved a bit north where wading is the only option for hikers. There is a usable log to the north a couple hundred yards, but that leaves you on the west side, where a cliff comes down to the stream edge. There are some stepping stones along here, but you still may have to step in the water a time or two. South of the regular crossing there was at one time a pile of debris that you may still be able to use for crossing. Almost immediately after crossing the creek you will find the Hermosa Creek Trail. Take it to the left gently uphill for three miles to its start, where your extra car should be parked. The climb out provides more than 300 feet of elevation gain, well spread out over the entire distance—just a pleasant hike.

Jones Creek Trail

Distance: *4.3 miles (one way)*
Starting elevation: *7,800 feet*
Elevation gain: *1,550 feet*
High point: *9,350 feet*
Rating: *Moderate*
Time allowed: *4 to 6 hours*
Maps: *7.5' Hermosa; San Juan National Forest; Durango
   Area Recreation Map*

Jones Creek Trail is an old trail that has been newly rebuilt and partially rerouted. The old trail was deeply rutted and was not pleasant in some places. The new one is delightful, mostly in big timber, ponderosa pine, fir, and spruce, with a small meadow at its terminus. It is located in much the same area as Hermosa Trail.

To reach the trailhead, follow the description for reaching the Hermosa Trail. Jones Creek trailhead turns right, uphill off the Hermosa Trail road about 200 yards before it ends at the beginning of the Hermosa Creek trailhead.

The trail climbs rather rapidly through switchbacks at first and then straightens out quite a bit for the rest of its length with some nice, flat areas. The trees are high enough and close enough in some places to give an air of mystery. The abundance of shade makes it a good hot-weather hike.

The new trail is popular with bikers, who can pop around sharp corners suddenly. All mountain bikers I have met are very courteous and typically slow down immediately.

With more than eight miles in the round trip, many hikers will be satisfied by just going out and back, but several other options are available for those who want a longer hike.

Pinkerton-Flagstaff Trail goes along the top of the ridge east of Jones Creek. This is the spine of the main high ridge east of Hermosa Creek, which lies to the west. The trail runs along much of the top west above the Hermosa Cliffs, with the

Animas River to the east. There is a lot of wild, roadless area between these two streams. On the ridge, the trail spends most of its length higher than 9,400 feet, going up to 9,661 feet at one point.

The Jones Creek Trail's most northerly point is its intersection with Pinkerston-Flagstaff. Left on this trail takes you in several miles up to Dutch Creek Trail. The right fork is more practical—in 2.6 miles, it curves southeast and parallels Jones Creek at a higher level and at a gradually widening distance. In this distance, it intersects the trail coming up from Mitchell Lakes and the east side of the major ridge. The top of the ridge has quite a bit of open space, presenting long-distance views into the high peaks of the La Plata Mountains to the west and to the top of Missionary Ridge to the east. It is a good place to take a well-earned rest from the climb and drink in the splendor of nature's best. You could get down to U.S. 550 in another 4.4 miles. See the Mitchell Lakes Trail description below for this east side.

Mitchell Lakes

Distance: *8 miles (round trip) to top of the ridge above the lakes*
Starting elevation: *6,800 feet*
Elevation gain: *2,600 feet*
High point: *9,400 feet*
Rating: *Moderate*
Time allowed: *4.5 to 5.5 hours*
Maps: *7.5' Hermosa; San Juan National Forest*

Mitchell Lakes as such are not much to brag about. There are four little lakes in the group. They are shallow and filled with marsh grass, but they occupy a secluded shelf surrounded by meadow, which, in turn, is surrounded by ponderosa pine and some aspen. There are perhaps a hundred acres of open space; here you can get a feeling of both spaciousness and insulation

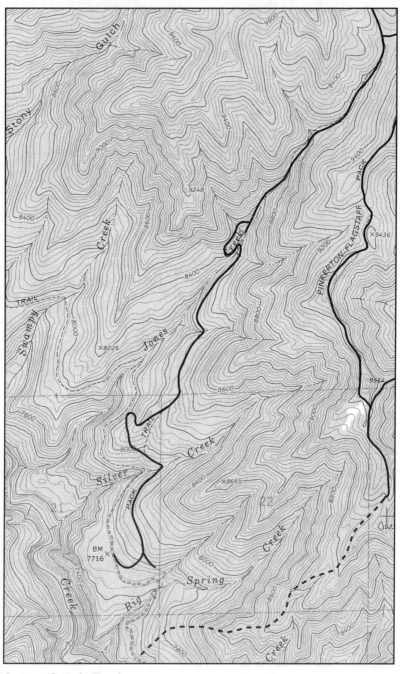

Jones Creek Trail

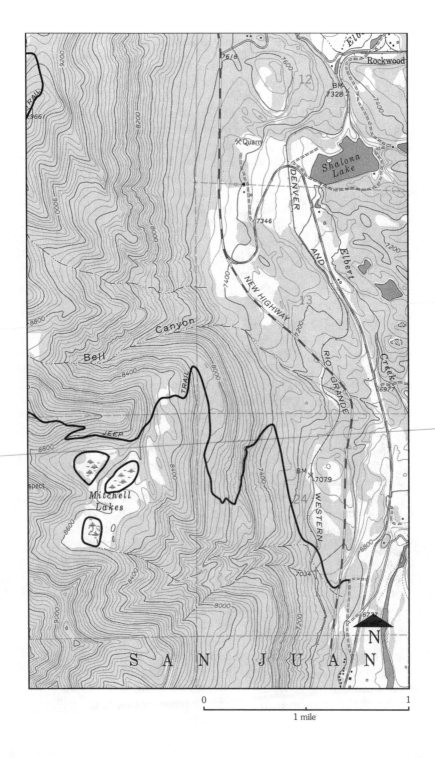

0   1

1 mile

from the rest of the world. The hike itself yields rewarding views of the Animas Valley and Missionary Ridge beyond.

To take this hike, follow U.S. Highway 550 thirteen miles north of Durango to a right turn downhill toward Baker's Bridge. You soon come to the old highway. Turn left on it (north) a little way to the first left turn. This is a dirt road and leads back west under the highway through a large steel tube. This soon becomes a very rough four-wheel-drive road. In fact, a four-wheel-drive vehicle could go all the way to the lakes, but it is not recommended since the road is very rough and, in places, very steep. It is one of the worst anywhere. It is preferable to park back on the old highway or just off it before going under the new highway.

Begin hiking at this point. You soon cross the narrow-gauge Durango-to-Silverton railroad track. Follow the road all the way to the lakes area, which is three miles. The lakes themselves are private property; if you keep to the road at the north side of the lakes you will be on public property. The road is closed to automotive travel about the place where it arrives at the east side of the lakes, but it goes on to the top of the ridge as a trail. The lakes are very shallow, but they add a nice touch to the scene in their open-meadow surroundings, a kind of respite from the heavy timber and steep road both below and above them.

At the top of the ridge, you strike the Pinkerton-Flagstaff Trail going north and south along the top of the ridge. (See the Jones Creek Trail description for the north part of this and for the way down to the Hermosa Trail Road via the Jones Creek Trail.) There are excellent views both east and west from the top. If you want to go back the way you came, you will have eight miles of good hiking through variable terrain—a good half day's hike.

The other option is to go down the west side with another car parked near the beginning of the Hermosa Trail. There are two ways to do this. Turn right at the top, and you will have a good trail all the way, mostly downhill, but it will be about seven miles. Turn left at the top, and you can be down to the road in two, but more adventuresome, miles. The first three-tenths mile is on trail, but it quits, and the rest of the hike is a bushwhack that must be navigated. I have done this route twice and rather liked it over the much longer alternative. To do this, follow the crest of the ridge to where it begins to go down; stay with the crest until it disappears in a steeper descent. Spring Creek will be the first drainage off to the right and will be quite some distance down at first. Cliff Creek is a smaller drainage to the left. Follow the highest part of the ridge on down to the road between these two drainages. Most of the time you will be in timber with a few open places. In a few spots there will be small, low brush, which can be a nuisance. There will also be a fairly steep descent of about 200 yards not very far from the bottom. This will bring you to the road below the Hermosa Creek trailhead perhaps as much as a quarter mile. Therefore, some bias to the right would be useful if that is where you parked your second car.

Goulding Creek

Distance: *6 miles (round trip)*
Starting elevation: *7,880 feet*
Elevation gain: *2,190 feet*
High point: *10,070 feet*
Rating: *Moderate*
Time allowed: *3.5 to 4.5 hours*
Maps: *7.5'Electra Lake; San Juan National Forest*

Ten miles north of Durango a series of high bluffs begins on the west side of U.S. Highway 550. These bluffs, known as Hermosa Cliffs, continue on north for sixteen miles. In places they are precipitous and look invulnerable. But they can be breached via three good trails. Near the south end, ahead of the genuine cliffs, is the Mitchell Lakes Trail; near the middle is Goulding Creek; and near the north end is Elbert Creek.

Goulding approaches from an area that looks nearly impossible from below, but it turns out to be a very good trail and not terribly steep, thanks to many switchbacks. It is a trail satisfactory for horses. Horse-riding hunters use it in the fall and cattlemen through the summer.

The trail is located seventeen miles north of Durango and leads off U.S. Highway 550. The trail is about one mile north of the main gate of the Tamarron resort on the opposite (west) side

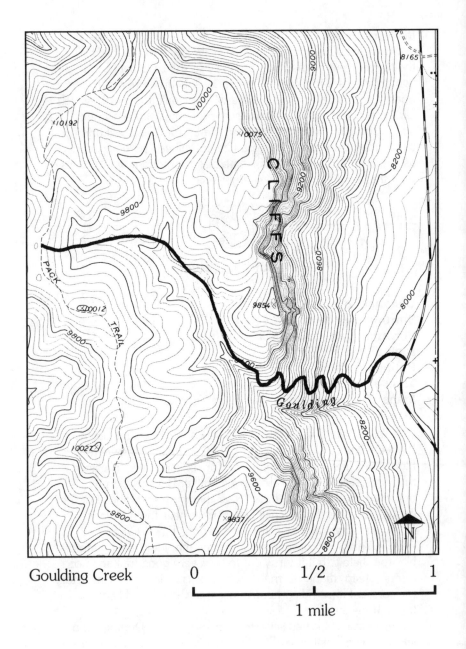

Goulding Creek

0   1/2   1

1 mile

of the road. You take a turnoff here where you can drive in a quarter-mile to grassy parking. The trail starts west looking like a four-wheel-drive road, but it quickly narrows to a trail and swings south above Tamarron's water supply tank. It soon moves westward again and mounts rapidly through a series of switchbacks up through a beautiful aspen grove. At some points, there are open spots in the trees that provide good views of the valley below and Missionary Ridge beyond. This is a beautiful hike at any time, but it is especially lovely during late September and early October, when the aspen leaves are at their golden best.

This trail is always slightly above Goulding Creek until you break through the Hermosa Cliffs at about one mile up the trail and a thousand feet of altitude gain.

When you get through the cliffs, you are ushered into a peaceful green valley surrounded by tall timber on the hillsides. This is only a mile from the highway (less in a straight line), but it is a different world, one inhabited by curious Herefords and freedom-loving elk and deer. A couple of old log cabins are located in the valley. One is a cattleman's line camp, and the other a shelter sometimes used by cattle.

You soon come close to the stream after arriving in the valley, but the water is not recommended for drinking without purification, unless you are early enough in the summer to be ahead of the cows. Goulding Creek during much of the summer is just a trickling stream; it sometimes ceases to flow altogether.

For a short hike, you could terminate here, but it is worth going on. The trail beyond is a little harder to follow because of the many cow paths, but with a bit of care you should not have much trouble. The main trail stays fairly close to the stream most of the time, moving northwest to the top of the ridge, where it ends by joining the Pinkerton-Flagstaff Trail, a north-south trail at the crest of the ridge. This is between Dutch Creek and Jones Creek.

The last quarter-mile to the top is surrounded by acres and acres of lupine. During much of the summer, beginning quite early, this is a sea of blue floral display, well worth the hike by itself.

At the top, you look westward down into the Dutch Creek drainage and on across the vast Hermosa Creek roadless area. This is one of the best elk summering grounds in southwest Colorado.

The three miles given in the heading presupposes a return back down the same trail. But those who want a long hike have a couple of other options. Either of these would mean coming out at or near the end of the Hermosa Road, where you would need another car or someone to pick you up, for you would be nearly fifteen miles by road from the original parking place.

The first and shortest route is to go left down Jones Creek Trail. To do this, first follow Pinkerton-Flagstaff left for three miles to the beginning of the Jones Creek Trail and take Jones Creek on down another 4.3 miles to the Hermosa Road, joining the road below its upper end. Or, instead of going to the Hermosa Road you could skip the Jones Creek route: Go south beyond its start on Pinkerton-Flagstaff another two miles and head down the Mitchell Lakes Trail on the east side. This would reduce the highway distance between parking places to only five miles.

The second option is via the Dutch Creek Trail. The easy but long way to join this trail is to go right (north) up the Pinkerton-Flagstaff Trail two miles to where the Dutch Creek Trail joins it from the west. It is about six and one-half miles down this trail to the Hermosa Trail and another five miles down (left, or southeast) that trail to the Hermosa Road.

Elbert Creek

Distance: *8 miles (round trip)*
Starting elevation: *8,800 feet*
Elevation gain: *1,650 feet*
High point: *10,450 feet*
Rating: *Easy, but long*
Time allowed: *4 to 6 hours*
Maps: *7.5′ Electra Lake; 7.5′ Elk Creek; San Juan National Forest*

The Elbert Creek Trail breaks through the Hermosa Cliffs four miles south of Purgatory Ski Area, or twenty-three miles north of Durango on U.S. Highway 550. The trailhead is a little

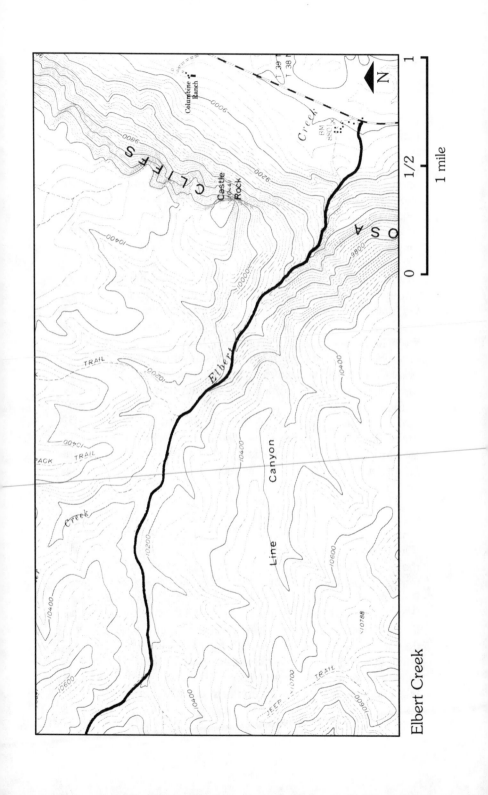

Elbert Creek

difficult to locate, but the trail soon becomes well defined beyond its beginning. It starts just south of the boundary of Needles Country Store and goes west along the south side of a fence through a narrow corridor of private property that brings you to the national forest boundary in a couple of hundred yards. In another 300 yards you come to Elbert Creek. During the spring snowmelt it can be a good-sized stream and a problem for crossing. You may elect just to wade it; later on in the summer it may be completely dry. It has to be crossed again higher up, but this first crossing is the only difficult one.

The hike is not difficult. The trail rises through some long switchbacks and soon enters a deep canyon that makes its way through the Hermosa Cliffs and climbs quite gradually through big timber in four miles to the top of the ridge that separates this drainage from the Hermosa drainage. It is a good trail most of the way. At one point it joins and follows a road for a few hundred yards. It follows along the south side of the creek at this point. You should be able to pick it up again where the road turns north to cross the creek. It is another one and a half miles to the top of the ridge.

This hike description only takes you to the top of the ridge; the return is by the same route. The trail, however, turns south along the top and eventually follows Little Elk Creek down to the Hermosa Trail in six miles. This route is not recommended unless you are prepared to stay overnight.

The road that you cross before reaching the top of the ridge is a good dirt road. It is possible to terminate the hike there, only three miles from its beginning. This road is reached from the Purgatory Ski Area. To get to it, turn off U.S. Highway 550 at the ski area turnoff. Just as you arrive at the east end of the Purgatory parking area, turn right; this road goes above Purgatory in a series of switchbacks to the top of the ridge. Where this road turns right in a flat spot, take a left turn instead. In about five miles of twisting road you come to the spot where the Elbert Creek Trail joins it. This road is on the whole pretty good, and two-wheel-drive vehicles can use it when it is dry, though there are a few rough spots. Those who want an easy hike could drive to this point and hike down.

Forebay Lake

Distance: *3 miles (round trip)*
Starting elevation: *8,120 feet*
Elevation gain: *160 feet*
High point: *8,280 feet*
Rating: *Easy*
Time allowed: *1.5 hours*
Maps: *7.5'Electra Lake*

This is a very easy hike, with little elevation change, along a four-wheel-drive road. It passes through rather dense vegetation, which makes it a bit unique in this part of the state. Forebay Lake is a good fishing place. It has been a supply lake for Tacoma power plant but is currently being bypassed for that purpose.

To get to the starting point for this hike, take U.S. Highway 550 eighteen miles north of Durango to a right turn (east) on the Haviland Lake Road. Haviland Lake is a lovely larger lake with a nice forest service campground and good fishing. Drive in from the highway about a mile; shortly after crossing the bridge at the southeast corner of Haviland you should be able to find parking room. Four-wheel-drive vehicles could drive all the way to Forebay Lake, but the road is too rough for other vehicles. Anyway, it is a lovely hike.

After parking, continue hiking east from Haviland. A road goes north here, but that leads up into the camping area. Along much of the hike you will be following a big pipe that carries the water supply for Tacoma from Electra Lake, a mile farther north. (Electra Lake is a large and attractive place but is not open to the public.)

Just southeast of Forebay you can stand at the top of the bluff overlooking the Animas River and the power plant a thousand feet below. At the right time of day in the summer you might even see the little narrow-gauge train at the bottom of the canyon carrying sightseers between Durango and Silverton.

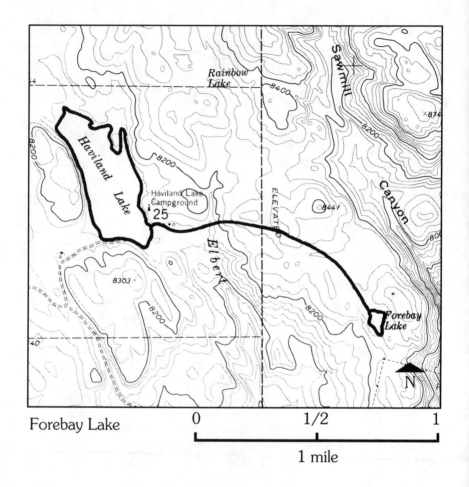

Forebay Lake

0   1/2   1

1 mile

Across the Animas Valley the view is up the steep, high western side of Missionary Ridge.

The road stops at Forebay, so the return must be made back up the way you came.

Molas Trail

Distance: *8 miles (round trip)*
Starting elevation: *10,604 feet*
Elevation gain: *1,674 feet*
High point: *10,604 feet*
Rating: *Easy to moderate*
Time allowed: *3.5 to 4.5 hours*
Maps: *7.5′ Snowden Peak; San Juan National Forest*

This is a good trail and offers a very fine half-day hike with excellent views of the Animas Canyon. Most hikes in this guide start at the low point and climb to a high point. This hike is the opposite; it starts at the high point and goes down to the low point at the river, which is at 8,930 feet. The elevation gain is on the return trip.

This trail starts off the east side of U.S. Highway 550 about six miles south of Silverton, one and one-half miles north of Molas Pass. There is a good turnout with a parking area south of Molas Lake (not to be confused with Little Molas Lake, one-half mile farther south and on the west side of the road). You could also enter the trail from Molas Lake itself. This is a privately operated recreational spot that offers camping, fishing, and sup-plies. From here you would reach the trail by going south along the lake until you strike the main trail going east.

The actual trailhead is across the road from the main park-ing area; the trail moves south, curving eastward in a quarter-mile past a sheep camp and down a hill. As soon as you cross the low point, usually a dry stream, there is some difficulty following the trail. If you continue east with some bias to the south, you should pick it up again moving over a little rise. Molas Creek should be several hundred yards to the right (as you face east). The trail is distinct down through the rocky east side of this rise. It leads down and eastward across an open meadow with an aspen grove on the left. If you are in the aspens, you will need to move south down a steep slope covered with aspen. At the bottom, the trail is quite distinct and is excellent the rest of the way to the river.

After crossing the flat meadow, you plunge into big spruce-fir timber. Shortly, the trail begins a series of switchbacks leading down to the river, 1,000 feet below. Here and there a break in the trees affords a dramatic view of the canyon below. The river winds its way through the bottom, with the railroad track paralleling it on the east side.

Mount Garfield stands stalwart guard above the east side of the valley, while farther south the peak Fourteen massif seems to block off the whole canyon and reach all the way to the sky. In midafternoon you have a good chance of seeing one of the tourist trains seeking its way south toward Durango. At the south end of the visible part of the valley the train often stops to take on backpackers from Elk Creek.

There are several gorgeous views of the valley from different levels as you swing back and forth in your descent. At the bottom you cross Molas Creek and soon emerge from the high vegetation to find a fine bridge across the Animas River for hikers and horses.

This is the destination point for the hike described here, since this guide does not cover the Weminuche Wilderness. But if you are backpacking, you can cross the railroad track and go down a little to find the Elk Creek Trail up the east side of the canyon and to the top of the Continental Divide in another 8.2 miles.

For this hike, it is a matter of turning around and going back the way you came, and, of course, this is where the work begins as you ascend what you came down so easily. However, the climb out of the canyon can be rated easy to moderate because none of the many switchbacks are steep.

The Molas Trail is an old trail that is now incorporated into the Colorado Trail, leading all the way from Durango to Denver—474 miles. You can, if you like, begin this hike now from U.S. 550 near the top of Molas Pass. There is a nice overlook turnout there and some parking. This parking, however, is

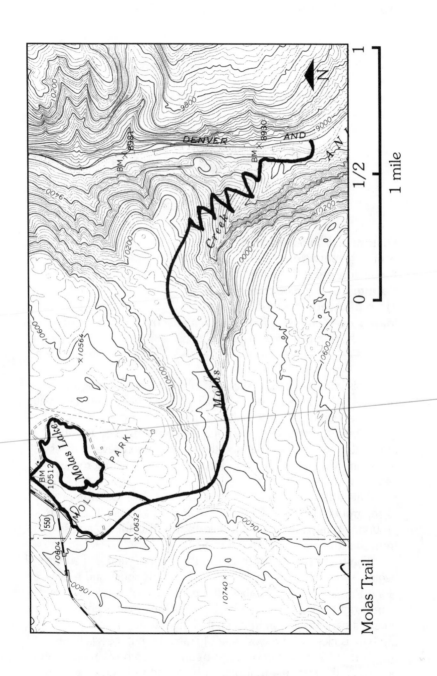

Molas Trail

better left for passing traffic rather than occupied for the many hours hikers will be gone. Also, if you do park there, you have a steep climb up the Colorado Trail on the return trip to reach your parking spot. You can avoid this by using the main parking area above the lake.

Purgatory Trail

Distance: *8 miles (round trip)*
Starting elevation: *8,800 feet*
Elevation gain: *1,100 feet*
Rating: *Easy to moderate*
Time allowed: *3.5 to 4.5 hours*
Maps: *7.5' Engineer Mountain; 7.5' Electra Lake; San Juan National Forest*

This hike is another reverse climb: You begin at the top, hike down to the river below (at 7,700 feet), then climb back out of the canyon. It's a good half-day hike, but the views, which are great by many standards, are not quite so dramatic as those afforded by the Molas Trail into the same canyon several miles upstream. Cascade Canyon is deep and narrow with a rugged beauty all its own.

This trail starts out of the northeast side of the Purgatory Campground. Parking is available near the highway. The campground is located twenty-eight miles north of Durango across from the Purgatory Ski Area turnoff.

The trail moves eastward from the campground and soon begins to descend rapidly. In one mile it turns south and moves along Purgatory Flats for about three-quarters of a mile, where it comes right along Cascade Creek just as the creek is about to enter its narrow canyon in its final plunge to the river. Most of the hike is close to the west side of Cascade, but it sometimes moves up to 250 feet above the stream in search of an adequate bench. At the end, the trail zigzags back and forth down to the

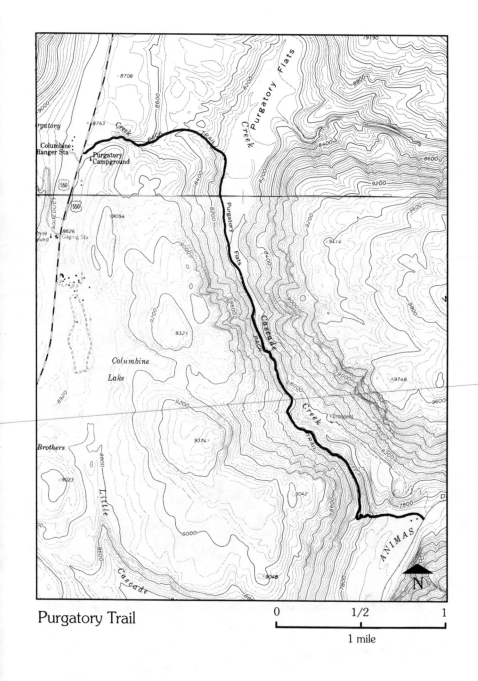

Purgatory Trail

0   1/2   1

1 mile

Looking out of Cascade Canyon along Purgatory Trail with Engineer Mountain in the distance.

river just below the mouth of Cascade Creek. Here is a nice flat area on both sides of the river for resting and picnicking. The east side is larger than the west and has some good tree coverage. There is a good bridge for hikers and horses.

At this point, the planned half-day hike returns back up the same trail. The trail itself, for backpackers, continues north along the east side of the river, always near to it, for another five and one-half miles, where it joins the Columbine Pass Trail. This, in turn, takes you on up to Chicago Basin and Columbine Pass.

This is an easy to moderate hike, but does have over a thousand feet of altitude gain on the return.

Potato (Spud) Lake

Distance: *2 miles (round trip)*
Starting elevation: *9,360 feet*
Elevation gain: *440 feet*
High point: *9,800 feet*
Rating: *Easy*
Time allowed: *1 hour*
Maps: *7.5' Engineer Mountain; San Juan National Forest*

Spud Lake is a short, easy hike, and a rewarding one. It is reached via U.S. Highway 550 about thirty miles north of Durango. At the bottom of Coal Bank Hill, just after crossing Cascade Creek, turn right on Lime Creek Road and go three and one-half miles to where the road passes a lily pond. Just as the road turns sharply east to go by the north side of the pond, there is a turnoff big enough to park two or three cars. The trail begins there and weaves around in a northerly direction. Some new parts of the trail were built in 1990 to decrease the grade in some steep spots. One hundred yards in, the new trail cuts off sharply to the right and rejoins the old route higher up. The trail passes through aspen trees and, shortly before the lake, goes past several interesting beaver ponds, some still active.

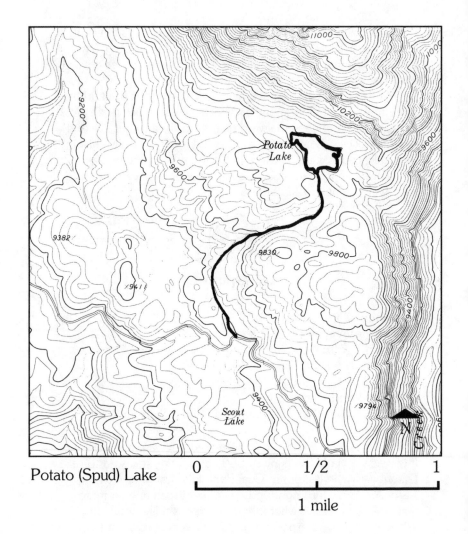

Potato (Spud) Lake

Spud Lake with large beaver lodge and a view of the south side of Spud Mountain.

The lake is officially named Potato Lake. Rising as a steep cliff out of the north side of the lake is Potato Hill. They are known popularly as Spud Lake and Spud Mountain. The lake provides several acres of good fishing. It is a lovely spot, with Spud Mountain very close on the north, the Twilight Peaks to the east across Lime Creek, and Engineer Mountain to the northwest. Engineer cannot be seen from the lake, but it can be viewed from several points along the trail. This is a beautiful hike during the summer, but it is especially beautiful during the early fall, when the aspen leaves are in full color. This is usually around October 1, but the colors are likely to be good ten days before and after this date.

There is another smaller but beautiful lake nearby (it is unnamed) for those who have time to explore a little more. To find it, start up the same trail from the parking lot; instead of turning right at 100 yards on the new trail, follow the old trail for two-tenths of a mile (count from the parking area). At that point the old Spud Lake Trail swings to the right and starts up steeply; for the other lake, turn left at this point on an old road and follow it generally west and gradually downhill for about a half-mile to a nice opening where the lake and surrounding meadow are located. It is a lovely quiet spot, not often visited.

Lime Creek Road is rocky in places but can be driven in a two-wheel-drive if you go carefully. This road is lovely all the way around to its north terminus, at the lowest spot between Coal Bank Pass and Molas Pass on U.S. Highway 550.

Potato Hill (Spud Mountain)

Distance: *3 miles (round trip)*
Starting elevation: *10,030 feet*
Elevation gain: *1,841 feet*
High point: *11,871 feet*
Rating: *Difficult*
Time allowed: *3 hours*
Maps: *7.5' Engineer Mountain; San Juan National Forest*

Spud Mountain is short compared to its neighbors, Engineer Mountain to the west and the Twilight Peaks and West Needles to the east, but it stands alone and makes a good half-day hike. The view south from the top is impressive. It includes the Cascade and Animas valleys and Electra Lake far below. Purgatory Ski Area is to the southwest.

Spud Mountain is best climbed from the west or north. This is bushwhacking most of the way on either route, through large spruce and fir. There are traces of trail near the top that other hikers and elk have used.

The west approach starts about one mile west of the peak at a hairpin turn on U.S. Highway 550, thirty-three miles north of Durango. There is adequate parking just above the hairpin turn on the west side of the road. Hikers should start eastward and aim for the rocky area just north of the top. The last several hundred yards contain some exposure and involve some interesting rock scrambling.

The north approach is about twice as long as the west route but has the advantage of starting at a higher altitude. For this route, park in the area at the top of Coal Bank Pass at 10,600 feet and strike out along the ridge toward the peak; it is basically south with a few degrees bias eastward. Again, it requires bushwhacking most of the way, with pieces of a trail available now and then. The last few hundred yards will be on rocks—the same route used from the west approach.

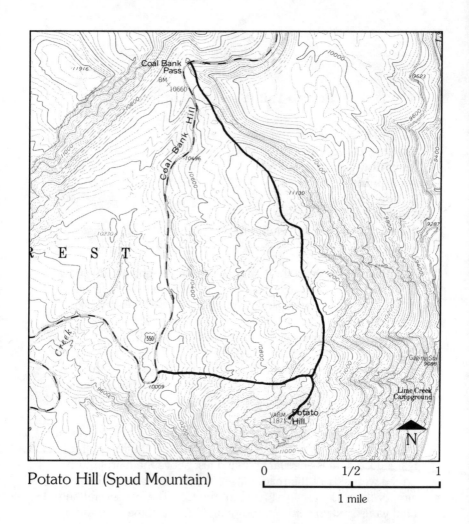

Potato Hill (Spud Mountain)

*Spud Mountain from the northwest, showing the highway just below
Coal Bank Pass.*

For those experienced climbers who would like a challenging
climb, this mountain can be done from the north side of Spud
Lake. (For the access route, see the Spud Lake hike description
on page 137.) This route is very steep, but a way can be picked
out from the lake nearly straight up by taking advantage of some
sloping ledges. You should aim for the east side of the rocky cliffs
that form the east side of the mountain near the top. Once at the
cliffs, you will need to go north a little below their base and
above the timber for roughly a quarter-mile to where they give
way to steep talus. Climb this west or southwest, depending on
where you choose to try; it is a short distance to the ridgeback.
Turn left and climb southwest to the summit. There are some
small trees located inconveniently along very narrow parts of the
ridge, but the top itself is grassy and large enough for a comfortable viewing and resting spot. The views in all directions make it
well worth the effort of the climb.

Engineer Mountain

Distance: *4.4 miles (round trip)*
Starting elevation: *10,660 feet*
Elevation gain: *2,308 feet*
High point: *12,968 feet*
Rating: *Difficult*
Time allowed: *4 to 5 hours*
Maps: *7.5′ Engineer Mountain; San Juan National Forest*

Engineer Mountain is one of the most photographed peaks in the San Juans. It is reached by U.S. Highway 550 between Durango and Silverton. As you approach from Durango about ten miles south of the peak, it appears as a symmetrical cone rising straight ahead as if out of the highway. From Jarvis meadows just north of the Purgatory Ski Area turnoff, it totally dominates the northerly view.

The shortest and easiest climb begins at the top of Coal Bank Pass. Just north of the large parking area located there, turn in on the opposite side of the road (west), going a little under 200 yards to the trailhead, labeled "Pass Creek Trail." There is parking here for a few cars. Start hiking north on the trail. It moves up a steep grassy slope northeastward into the big spruce-fir timber. Once inside the timber, it swings back gradually westward. Some new trail has been built recently in this area to improve the grade and to avoid some of the muddy spots. Two lovely little lakes lie on the left side of the trail. At about one and one-half miles, the trail emerges out of the timber onto the tundra. At this point, hikers should leave the trail and head directly for the northeast ridge of the mountain. The tundra area here has many beautiful wildflowers. As you move up the beginning of the cone, the tundra rises steeply, later giving way to rock—mostly talus with a few small ledges. Take the right side of the ridge at first, then move up onto the ridge itself.

The ridge is narrow—two to four feet wide in places. Much of the rock is loose, and there is much exposure here. Therefore,

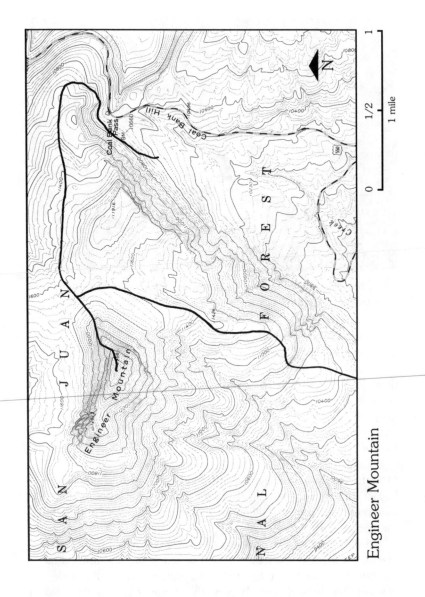

Engineer Mountain

The climbing route up the northeast ridge of Engineer Mountain rises out of the tundra.

you must test each handhold before trusting it. A little higher up you emerge out on the cone itself. The top is not far beyond.

Since Engineer stands alone, even though it is a little less than 13,000 feet, the panorama of peaks and valleys to be seen is great in all directions. The north face of Engineer is a sheer drop of 800 feet. Looking down this direction, you can see a fine example of a rock glacier at the head of one of the branches of Engine Creek.

Rock glaciers are somewhat unique to the San Juan Mountains. They look like a giant pudding flowing in slow waves. In fact, they are talus rocks that do move in a very slow pattern. Geologists say they are taken for a slow ride by ice in and under the rock.

If you have an extra couple of hours, you might want to go west from the top, over the small shoulder peak, and around to the north side and back to the tundra and trail across the rock glaciers. The west descent beyond the shoulder is over steep talus but is quite usable. Hiking the waves themselves involves some up-and-down work, all on loose rocks. You must be especially careful crossing leading edges of the waves, since the rocks are typically at the maximum angle of repose; hiking over them can start a hazardous rockslide. At several places along this area you can hear underground streams gurgling through the rocks.

San Juan National Forest gives the name Engineer Mountain Trail to an approach from the south. It is more than twice as long as the Coal Bank Pass route and involves 3,920 feet of altitude gain. This is a favorite trail for elk hunters in the fall. Hikers might be interested in it as an alternate or a return route, keeping in mind that the south end of it joins U.S. Highway 550 some five miles down from Coal Bank Pass. This trail is in good condition, having been rebuilt recently with some improvements to the route. It offers some fine views southward from several open meadows. To take it from Engineer Mountain look for a north-south trail crossing along the base of the east side of the cone. Going south, it soon drops into heavy timber and goes mostly south four miles to a junction with a little road 200 yards west of Highway 550. There used to be an electrical substation located here, which made the spot easy to find. Now if you want to start up this route from the south end, you need to measure up one mile from where the highway crosses Cascade Creek and turn left for that 200 yards. Or from the north it is the first right turn a little way below the runaway-truck turnoff. This road terminates at a national forest guard station. The trail starts north from the road a hundred yards before the station. You can park at the station or nearer the trailhead. Only 100 yards up the trail it splits. The route to the top goes north and soon into the woods. The route west is Cascade Trail. This is a new route for that trail. It starts west and then swings north, bypassing the cabin area in the bottom of Cascade Creek Valley before dropping into the valley and going on north toward South Mineral Creek on a route west of Engineer Mountain and east of Grizzly Peak.

Grizzly Peak

Distance: *7 miles (round trip)*
Starting elevation: *11,000 feet*
Elevation gain: *2,738 feet*
High point: *13,738 feet*
Rating: *Difficult; hard by alternate return route*
Time allowed: *6 to 7 hours*
Maps: *7.5' Ophir; 7.5' Engineer Mountain; San Juan National Forest*

Grizzly Peak is a challenging and rewarding climb. It rises out of the west side of the Cascade Creek Valley five miles northwest of Engineer Mountain. It is ten miles back from the road and can only be seen from U.S. Highway 550 thirty miles north of Durango, between the Purgatory Ski Area turnoff and the Cascade Creek crossing. As you travel northward here, you can see its peak and steep east side up the Cascade Valley to the left and beyond Engineer Mountain. It can be climbed from Cascade Valley, but this is a long route and involves two days.

The easiest route is the one described here. For this approach, turn west on the ski area turnoff twenty-eight miles north of Durango. As you approach the ski area itself, go north up a little road at the east end of the parking lot. This road soon climbs back to the west and overlooks the ski area. At the top of the climb, the road turns north and descends slightly; in about one-half mile, the main road makes a ninety-degree turn left and heads downhill to Hermosa Park. You should go straight on past this turn for approximately another mile. At this point the road divides again; take the right turn uphill instead of the road straight ahead. You will now be moving east on a logging road that soon curves around to the north high on the shoulder of Graysill Mountain, with Cascade Creek far below and Engineer Mountain beyond to the northeast. You should go all the way to the end of the road—about eight miles. Some of this road

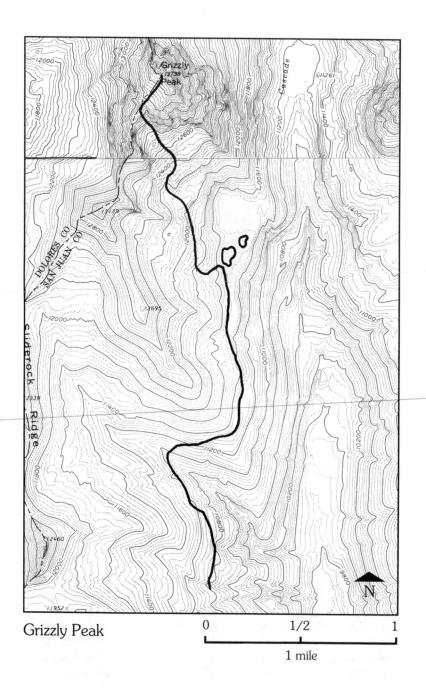

Grizzly Peak

Grizzly Peak; the trail goes around the base of the high foreground ridge.

requires a four-wheel-drive vehicle. Also, since it is a logging road, it is subject to possible cutoff by the forest service. If the road should be cut, it may still be better to hike to the end of the road than to take another route.

Park at the end of the road and walk on a well-defined path another quarter-mile to where you strike the Colorado Trail, which, at this point, is also the Rico-Silverton Trail (#507). (You should already have crossed the Graysill Trail on the road before this; don't make the mistake of taking it, for it descends into Cascade Creek instead of heading for Grizzly.) Assuming you are on the right trail, follow it north to a crossing of an unnamed creek, where the trail swings sharply right (eastward). At this point it is going around on a contour of a high, steep ridge that comes off the left side of Grizzly. Go on around the end of the ridge to where the trail begins to enter the woods and descend. Leave the trail here and continue on about the same contour level going straight north, nearly paralleling the trail. Your route will rise a little at times. There is no maintained trail here, but you may see evidence of a path that is used by other climbers. In about a mile you should come to a delightful shelf with some small lakes and marshy areas. A stream fills this area from

Grizzly Peak from across the Upper Cascade Canyon.

above, and another drains it, plunging over the side down to Cascade Creek.

At the southwest side of this area, climb steeply upward toward the northwest. Soon you should see a steep chute of big rocks with cliffs on each side. The right side of this is a shoulder of Grizzly Peak, the top of which you cannot see from here. Climb the chute (northwest). It is somewhat tedious but better than the alternatives. At the top, you will find yourself on a rocky ridge; turn right for a fairly easy quarter-mile climb over talus to the top of the mountain. The top itself is very rocky, but it affords excellent views of many rugged peaks that lie between South Mineral Creek on the east and Trout Lake on the west. The near ones in this area (north) include, west to east, Sheep Mountain, San Miguel Peak, and Rolling Mountain. A bit farther north, to the left of Rolling Mountain, are Vermillion Peak and U.S. Grant Peak. Farther to the west and a little north are the San Miguel Mountains. These include three fourteeners: Wilson Peak, Mount Wilson, and El Diente, in addition to Lizard Head and its distinctive shaft rising 400 feet straight up out of the top of the mountain. An eastern view shows the many peaks around Silverton and, farther south, the rugged Needles area of the Weminuche Wilderness.

The climbing chute above the lakes on Grizzly Peak.

For the return trip, the same route is recommended. But for those interested in rock climbing, instead of taking the chute down to the marshy area, continue south along the ridge. This is farther and slower. On this route you will move up and down over various sizes of rocks. At times there is much exposure and slow rock climbing. The route is not recommended for the inexperienced or faint of heart. Once over this tricky ridge, climb to the highest point (still going south) and proceed down the steep south side to a more gentle tundra area. Hike southeast and back to the end of the road.

An alternate route from the one described starts near Bolam Pass. (Four-wheel-drive vehicles are advisable for this route, but when the road is good, high-clearance two-wheel-drives can make it; you do have to ford Hermosa Creek, which can be risky for two-wheel-drives in the early summer when the creek is still swollen with snowmelt.) For this route, take the main road above Purgatory Ski Area down into Hermosa Park. At its west end, the road turns north and follows Hermosa Creek up to its headwaters. About two miles up this road after leaving Hermosa Park there is a division in the road, with the left turn going to Hotel Draw and Scotch Creek; do not take this turn, but go straight on.

Eventually, you should come to the ghost town of Graysill, which was active in uranium mining in the 1940s and 1950s. Park here and hike northeast along the west side of the ridge leading to Grizzly. There is a trail much of the way. This route involves a very steep rocky climb up the west side of Grizzly. There is an unnamed peak a mile south of Grizzly. You will find it easier to climb over this peak from a saddle southwest of it than to climb directly up the west side of Grizzly. If you do this, you will then have to follow the tricky ridge, described above, on over to Grizzly.

Jura Knob (Coal Creek, Deer Creek)

Distance: *6.5 miles (loop trip)*
Starting elevation: *10,300 feet*
Elevation gain: *2,314 feet*
High point: *12,614 feet*
Rating: *Moderate*
Time allowed: *5 to 6 hours*
Maps: *7.5' Engineer Mountain; San Juan National Forest*

Coal Creek and Deer Creek trails provide fine half-day hikes into big timber, but I have combined them here into a very good full-day hike. The trailheads are both on U.S. Highway 550 and are about two miles apart; therefore, this highway distance will need to be provided for in hiking, or some other arrangements will have to be made. This is in addition to the time and mileage given above. Good parking space is available near both trailheads.

The easier way to do this hike is to begin at Coal Creek, since it is 500 feet higher. This high-altitude hike involves considerable altitude gain. Otherwise, it is easy, with only one spot (near the top) where rock scrambling is involved.

Coal Creek is the first drainage north of Coal Bank Pass. Just below where Highway 550 crosses the creek, park on the south side of the road and walk down the highway about 200 yards to where the trail starts sharply upward in a westerly direction in the bare highway cut. The trail soon angles northeast into

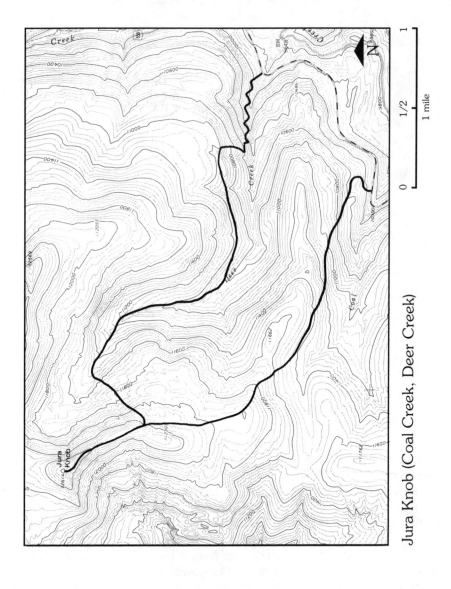

Jura Knob (Coal Creek, Deer Creek)

Jura Knob: The shoulder-high ledge is on the left side, Rolling Mountain is in the center, and the shoulder of Twin Sisters is on the right.

the trees, then curves back around westward. At about one and one-fourth miles, the trail emerges into a grassy clearing. Timberline can be seen a few hundred yards above this to the north. The trail itself continues westward to join the Engineer Mountain Trail. To climb Jura Knob, leave the trail, climbing northwest toward the highest point you can see in the clearing. This clearing is beautifully loaded with wildflowers. Upon reaching this high point, you can look northeastward across Deer Creek Valley, hundreds of feet below, to two peaks about the same size. Neither of these is Jura Knob. Continue to the northwest another half-mile upward and you will be on the beginning of an easy ridge leading directly north to Jura Knob, one mile beyond. One obstacle of some difficulty remains. It is a ledge a short distance below the top. Here there is one shoulder-high vertical climb. Most adults can make this by themselves with proper placement of the feet. Anyone can make it with a boost from a partner.

The top, lying a short distance beyond the ledge, is a smooth roll with small flat rocks for its surface. It is a good place to stretch out for a rest or to eat a sandwich while enjoying views of peaks in all directions. Immediately to the north are the Twin

Sisters on the right and Rolling Mountain to the left. Farther
north between these is the Ice Lakes area, with U.S. Grant Peak
immediately beyond. Ice Lake itself cannot be seen. To the west,
Grizzly Peak majestically guards over the Cascade Valley, but
there is a low ridge in between that keeps you from seeing down
into that valley. If you were to hike directly west, you would soon
strike the Highline Trail, now a part of the Colorado Trail, just
beyond the saddle in this ridge. This trail could be taken north to
South Mineral Creek Campground or south to the highway. Both
routes require several miles of hiking.

But the objective on this hike is to head back eastward
through Deer Creek. To do this, go back down over the shoulder-
high ledge. Just below it, you can drop down the steep hillside
northeast into Deer Creek through the scree and a stretch of
knee-high willows. It is easier to go back along the approach
ridge farther and drop down where the hillside is not so steep.
Most of the Deer Creek Trail lies on the east side of the creek,
although near the beginning of the creek you may find a bit of
trail on the west side. Assuming that you have not found it on
the west side, cross the creek, and you will find the trail a little
way beyond. The trail then follows down the creek, staying on
the east side near the creek a considerable distance. There is a
riot of wildflowers along this trail up to where it enters the heavily
wooded area. Inside the tall timber, the trail stays high as the
stream plunges rapidly downward. About a mile above the highway the trail again emerges into a clearing and zigzags rapidly
down to the highway 800 feet below, entering an aspen grove
just before its finish.

Deer Creek Trail, round-trip, makes a good half-day hike by
itself. There is a thousand-foot climb in the first mile, but it is a
good switchback trail. To find the trailhead from U.S. Highway
550: It is the second drainage north of Coal Bank Pass and the
second south of Molas Pass. Just north of the creek on the east
side of the highway is good parking space. About 150 yards
north of the parking area you should find the trail starting
upward. There is a sign to mark it.

Sultan–Grand Turk

Distance: *7.5 miles round trip (8 miles if Grand Turk is included)*
Starting elevation: *10,910 feet*
Elevation gain: *2,458 feet*
High point: *13,368 feet*
Rating: *Difficult*
Time allowed: *5.5 to 6.5 hours*
Maps: *7.5' Snowden Peak; 7.5' Silverton; San Juan National Forest*

This is a good climb, mostly above timberline; there are no really difficult spots. Most of it is on tundra and loose rock. It can include either Grand Turk or Sultan or both. The seven-and-one-half-mile round trip takes Sultan only and returns by a different route, but Grand Turk can easily be included.

The hike starts at Little Molas Lake. To get there, take U.S. Highway 550 six and one-half miles south of Silverton. This is forty-three miles north of Durango. The Little Molas Lake road is gravel and turns off Highway 550 west a mile south of Big Molas Lake and four-tenths of a mile north of Molas Pass. Little Molas cannot be seen from the highway. Follow this road about a mile to a point northwest of Little Molas, where it turns south. The trail begins here, but you may have to drive on south a little way to find a spot to park off the roadway.

The hike starts off uphill nearly straight north and passes through an open area caused by an ancient burn. There is a wide area of new planting of little trees to pass through. In some spots there is a pretty good trail, but missing it is no cause for concern. Continuing to climb north with a little bias to the west, you will soon get into an open, slowly rising basin with high craggy ridges on each side. Head toward the center of this, the low spot, and you will find a trail leading out the top of it. At the top, you will come to a small flat area and another peak straight ahead (north)

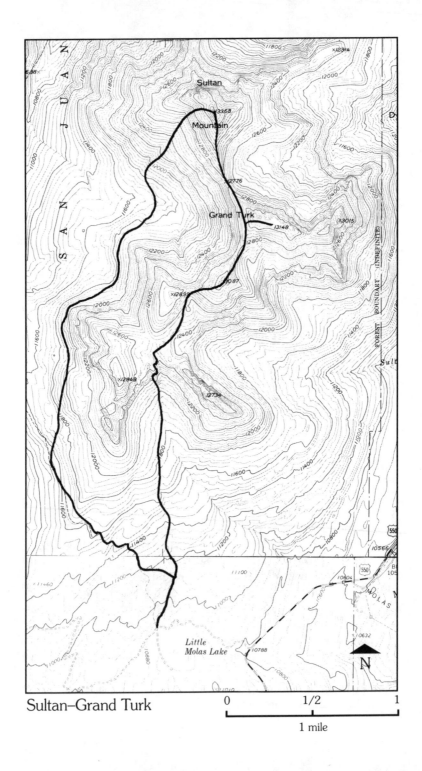

Sultan–Grand Turk

Grand Turk and Sultan mountains viewed across Silverton from the north.

rising about 500 feet. There is usually a path traversing the steep east side of this. Follow it on around another quarter-mile to a small saddle between this peak and another northeast of it. Climb up into the saddle and northeast over this peak. When you drop down to the next saddle (still headed northeast), you will have lost 300 feet. You are now at the base of Grand Turk.

To climb Grand Turk adds another half-mile to the seven and one-half miles listed in the heading. It is fairly easy to do, however. Just continue straight up the ridge, and where it begins to spread out a bit, veer off to the right. Grand Turk has trouble deciding where to peak out. Actually, it has three peaks close together that are about the same height. The topographic map labels the one farthest east at 13,148 feet and does not give heights for the others. Grand Turk also has twin peaks still a little farther east, but these are a hundred or more feet lower than the other three. These twin peaks are what you see as the distinctive split-topped mountain most frequently viewed from the highway and the train.

To continue on to Sultan, go back along the top of Grand Turk's ridge to a northwest descent along a fairly narrow ridge.

The long glissade route off Sultan's southwest side.

You will lose 370 feet down to the next saddle between Grand Turk and Sultan.

If you choose not to climb Grand Turk, follow along its west end a couple hundred feet below its top to the same saddle just mentioned. This point is at 12,776 feet. Follow up the ridge northwest to the top of Sultan at 13,368 feet.

Sultan provides a fine view northeast down on Silverton, 4,000 feet below. North is Anvil Mountain, which connects with Red Mountain. In the valley, U.S. Highway 550 leads on up toward Ouray. To the west below is Bear Creek, and just beyond is Bear Mountain (12,987 feet). Beyond this is Ice Lakes country, with many rugged peaks and ridges.

The return can be made by the same route or via an alternate. For the alternate, go west down the side of the cone. This looks pretty steep from above, but once on it, you will find it not too bad. You soon reach a steep drainage headed southwest down the mountainside. Follow down or near this to the basin below. Since the side of the mountain is mostly talus, patience and care are called for on this descent, but it is not difficult if you do not get too far south, where it is steeper. Actually, early in the season there is an excellent glissade possibility down this steep drainage. At the very top it is too steep for safety, but not far down you can begin and go nearly to the bottom much faster and easier than the tedious hiking over the rocks. This is the longest glissade I have ever taken—most of a mile long.

Once in the basin, contour around at first southwest and later more directly south. This will take you along the west side of the massif you climbed earlier. Continuing on around southeast, eventually you should be able to spot Little Molas Lake and go on down to the point of origin. Actually, if you stay a little low as you round the south end of the massif, you should strike the Colorado Trail coming from the west and headed for Little Molas. Take it to the road west of the lake; take this road to your parking spot.

Crater Lake–Twilight Peaks

Distance: *5.5 miles to Crater Lake; 1.2 miles more to North Twilight Peak; plus equal return mileage*
Starting elevation: *10,750 feet*
Elevation gain: *890 feet to Crater Lake; 1,435 feet additional to North Twilight*
High point: *11,640 feet at Crater Lake; 13,075 feet at North Twilight*
Rating: *Easy but long to Crater Lake; difficult to the peak*
Time allowed: *4 to 5 hours to Crater Lake; 2 hours additional to North Twilight (round trip times)*
Maps: *7.5' Snowden Peak; San Juan National Forest*

This is a combination hike with two possible destinations, both of which are highly worthwhile.

The trailhead is at Andrews Lake, which is reached via U.S. Highway 550 about eight miles south of Silverton. Andrews Lake is less than a mile southeast of the highway. The road to Andrews Lake turns off the highway a mile south of the summit of Molas Pass.

Park at Andrews Lake. The trail, which may be picked up on either the south or north side of the lake, moves east beyond the lake and soon turns south, zigzagging up 400 feet. After this, it continues south to Crater Lake, only rising sharply for short distances. The trail moves in and out of the edge of the timber, affording fine views northward toward the mountains surrounding Silverton and westward across Lime Creek Valley to Engineer Mountain and Grand Turk. The high spruce-fir bands of forest on both sides of this valley are excellent elk-hunting areas.

The last clearing where the trail turns east for a half-mile affords a distinctive view of the steep north face of the Twilight massif. About a mile beyond this you reach the lake, a lovely little high-altitude gem surrounded by tall trees; timberline is just above it.

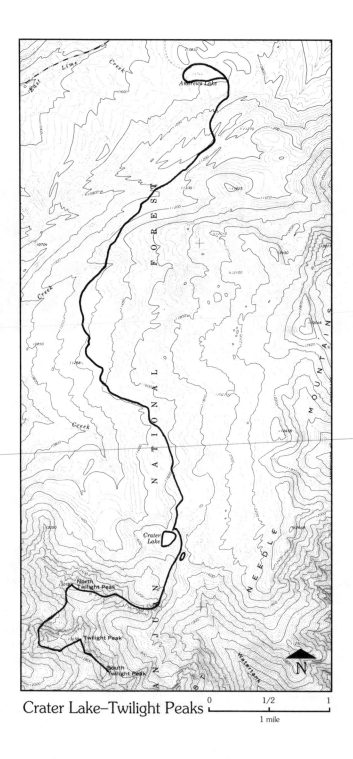

Crater Lake–Twilight Peaks

0   1/2   1

1 mile

The Twilight–West Needles massif from the open-meadow ascent of Jura Knob.

The hike into the lake and back can be done in a long half-day. Some may want to take advantage of the excellent camping sites here and perhaps do a little fishing and relaxing. The hike to Crater Lake and back is rated fairly easy, but it is long.

For those who would like to climb Twilight, the challenge has just begun, for the next mile brings steep climbing and one and a half times as much altitude gain as has already been made in five and one-half miles.

To begin the ascent, follow around the north side of the lake and start the climb eastward beyond the lake. There is no fixed trail beyond this point, but you should have no difficulty finding your way because you are out of the timber by this time. A few hundred yards southeast and 150 feet higher is another little lake. At this point, turn southwest and ascend steeply toward the peak. The first top is a false one; from it you must climb down a little. Be careful here, for there is considerable exposure in this little dip. Climb out of the dip to the top a quarter-mile beyond. The top itself is a smooth roll.

From the top, you can see to the east the rugged Needles territory where there are three 14,000-foot mountains as well as myriad other steep and rugged peaks. This is truly wilderness, roadless territory. Between Twilight and the Needles steeply below is the Animas River valley. If you are there at the right time of day, you might even hear the little Durango-Silverton train whistle its loneliness up and out of the valley.

North Twilight is part of a massif called the West Needle Mountains; this includes Snowdon Peak to the north and Twilight, South Twilight, and West Needle Mountains to the south. All of these peaks are in the 13,000-foot class. Hikers who have time and energy left after reaching North Twilight could take in Twilight and South Twilight in the next mile. Twilight (the middle of the Twilights) is actually the highest of the group at 13,158 feet. The drop between North Twilight and Twilight is only 400 feet; however, the hike between is not as simple as this sounds, for there is a deep gash on the west side of Twilight.

The gash is a serious problem. There are two possible routes, both bad, but in different ways. The easier route first: Descend farther south and west, cross a little gully, and move on ahead to where you begin to climb more easily toward the top of Twilight; after that summit, take another easy descent to the next saddle and then on up to the top of South Twilight. This sounds easy enough, but there is a hazard. As soon as you cross the gully, you are on a place a few feet wide; it drops off sharply on the right with no hand or footholds. There is risk of a very serious fall. But more problems—the little area on which you are standing slopes down toward the dropoff and is made up of a lot of small loose rocks. So what now? There is a rising ledge a few feet high on the left that offers some not-too-secure handholds. The tough part is only ten to twenty feet long. I tried it and had no trouble, but my two climbing partners refused to follow me without ropes and pitons for security. So I went on to climb both Twilight and South Twilight, while they waited patiently for more than an hour.

Then we started back, disappointed that two of the three had made only one of the three Twilight peaks. (I should add that they are excellent climbers with a lot of experience.) For another look, we went back up to the top of the gash. It drops straight down approximately eighty feet with no apparent way to make it without ropes, which we did not have. After a thorough search, they finally found a way to cross down and to the right of the highest part. Once at the bottom of the crevice, they found the climb out the other side steep but with good holds. This crossing spot is difficult to find, but it is there. My partners felt it was much safer than the way I went. So now *I* waited for them to finish Twilight and South Twilight—not too difficult the rest of the way. Then three tired but happy climbers made their way back several miles to their car.

The return trip is ordinarily made by the same route as the approach.

Hikers who like steep climbing might want to try bushwhacking directly up the west side of this massif instead of taking the long hike from Andrews Lake. This route would involve taking Lime Creek Road off U.S. Highway 550. At about the midpoint of this side loop there is a parking and picnic area, formerly maintained as a campground by the forest service. Lime Creek is a good-sized stream, usually with a complement of fishermen and picnickers. There is no trail on this route; it is only for the hardy. First you must wade the stream, fight your way through a short band of tangled brush, then move steeply upward. Twilight and North Twilight are only a little over a mile above the creek, but more than 4,000 feet of altitude must be gained in this distance. A drainage comes down between these two peaks with a nice little lake just below the peaks well above timberline. This route is rated very difficult.

Snowdon Peak

Distance: *6 miles (round trip)*
Starting elevation: *10,744 feet*
Elevation gain: *2,333 feet*
High point: *13,077 feet*
Rating: *Hard*
Time allowed: *5 hours*
Maps: *7.5′ Snowdon Peak; San Juan National Forest*

Snowdon is a twin-peaked mountain with each peak sloping gently toward the low point between. The two are quite symmetrical and make a distinctive skyline view eastward from U.S. Highway 550 as you travel toward the top of Molas Pass from

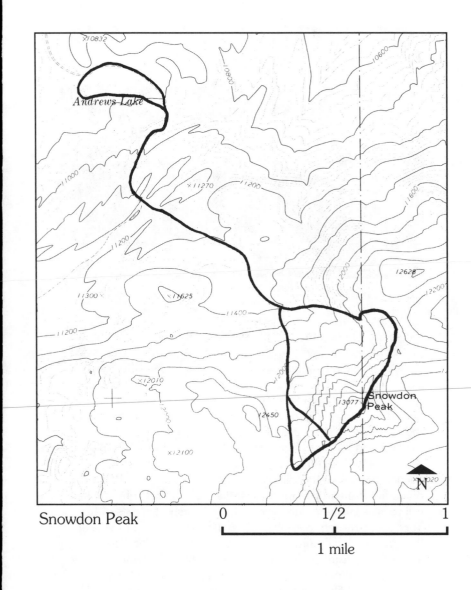

Snowdon Peak

0   1/2   1

1 mile

Snowdon Peak.

the south. Though the two peaks slope gently toward each other in a north-south direction, the view you get from the west side makes the climb look impossible. It is a steep slab 800 feet down from the top. Though this is not the route suggested here, the climb should still be rated hard.

The approach is the same as for Crater Lake–Twilight. Take the Andrews Lake road one mile south of Molas Pass. Park at the lake and hike east along either side of the lake. Turning south, you will find the trail zigzagging up a 400-foot rise; just beyond the top of this hill you will find two little lakes below you on your left. Here you must leave the trail; the rest of the hike will require bushwhacking except for a few short pieces of trail. Turn east between these two lakes. (At some times of the year they may be little more than swamps.) Cross a half-mile of flats and a slowly rising area. There is a smaller peak to the north of the most northerly of the Snowdon peaks. Contour upward through the timber toward this peak and above timberline a bit to the right to strike the saddle between this peak and the north

Snowdon peak. Continue up this ridge, now hiking south toward the top of Snowdon. Within a few hundred yards of the top, the rocks become too difficult on the face of the ridge. Here you should move to the east side of the ridge and climb south, finishing up southwest to the summit. There is substantial exposure in this last section. All handholds and footholds should be carefully tested before being trusted. Climbers may need to stay close together to help one another through this area. Rope could be used here, but most experienced climbers do not rope up for this short distance. The top itself widens out to a broad roll of small rocks. It is fairly large.

The views from the top include the Animas Valley steeply below to the east and the dramatic Grenadier Range straight east beyond. Mount Garfield is the first peak in the range. The Grenadiers are a favorite place for technical climbers. Straight north is Grand Turk on the west side of the highway and Sultan Mountain beyond. Just east of Sultan, on the right side of the valley, is Kendall Mountain, which is the peak that towers over the east side of Silverton. Beyond these is a grand panorama of many peaks.

Of the twin Snowdon peaks, the north one, which is the approach route described here, is the higher.

The return may be varied from the approach. Go south toward the low point between the two peaks. There is a break in the rock here, and you will have to do some rock scrambling to get down. At the bottom of this scramble you are faced with some interesting rock pylons. To the right is a steep couloir that can be used with care. Sometimes there is enough snow here for a good glissade, but the slope is steep, and ice axes are advisable for a possible arrest. A more gradual route down can be found by keeping to the left. Either route circles from west to north. At the bottom of this steep area (now 1,000 feet below the north peak), continue north or a little northwest to get back to the flat swampy area from which the approach was made. Westward across this will bring you back to the Crater Lake Trail again. Turn right on it to go back to Andrews Lake.

Graysill Mountain–Grayrock Peak

Distance: *6.3 miles (round trip)*
Starting elevation: *10,300 feet*
Elevation gain: *2,204 feet*
High point: *12,504 feet*
Rating: *Moderate*
Time allowed: *3.5 to 4.5 hours*
Maps: *7.5' Engineer Mountain; San Juan National Forest*

Graysill Mountain is a formation in the shape of a horse-shoe, facing east; it peaks out on its southeast corner, and at that point it is called Grayrock Peak. It is not a high peak compared to many of the others in the San Juans, but since it is the highest point for several miles in any direction, it is impressive and yields fine views. It is located west of Cascade Creek and southwest of Engineer Mountain.

Graysill lies north of Purgatory Ski Area. To reach it, take U.S. Highway 550 twenty-eight miles north of Durango and turn left (west) on the ski-area road. As you approach the ski area itself, go north up a little road at the east end of the parking lot. This road climbs in a series of switchbacks to the top of the ski slope. Here it turns north. In a half-mile there is a left turn down into Hermosa Park; do not take this, but go on for about a mile and turn right (east) uphill. Follow this road four and one-half miles. It swings eastward to the shoulder of Cascade Creek Canyon and then turns to the north. You eventually pass along the east shoulder of Graysill and can look up to your destination sharply above. The four and one-half miles bring you beyond Grayrock Peak to Pando Creek. Park in any wide spot near the creek. Three branches of Pando come together near the place where the road crosses the creek.

Start the hike west along the most northerly branch of the creek. The northern point of the horseshoe will be ahead and to your right. There is no trail here; bushwhacking is required, but it should not be too difficult. If you stay a bit to the right of the creek, you get out of the timber in a half-mile; if you stay near the stream, the timber carries on for a mile. At any rate, aim for a shallow saddle at the top of the drainage. Once here, you will find a relatively flat tundra area. To reach the peak, swing left for an easy 1.8 miles to the top. The saddle is nearly 800 feet below the peak, but the climb is gradual and therefore not difficult. The route goes south from the saddle and gradually curves more eastward, ending up almost straight east.

Grayrock Peak features its own special thrill—a sheer cliff on its north side practically straight down for a thousand feet. After recovering from the sight of this plunge, you will want to enjoy the more distant views. Engineer rises as a fine, stalwart warrior out of Cascade Canyon 3.8 miles northeast. Grizzly is a sharp and dominant point six miles north, even higher than Engineer. Eastward are the West Needles and the Twilight peaks. Northwest are Hermosa Peak and the Bolam Pass area. On the southwest skyline are the La Plata Mountains.

The return should be made by the same route as the climb. You could get down to the road and back to the parking spot in just over a mile by following the northeast ridge, but some of this is very steep; much of it is talus.

Grayrock can be climbed also from a western approach. This is actually easier than the route given above, but it is longer, and harder to find the starting point. The access road is the same until you are above Purgatory Ski Area. Instead of taking the right turn after you pass the turn that leads to Hermosa Park, go straight ahead. The road (F.S. 580) goes west and northwest, passing under the shoulder of Grayrock on the south side. The road is a good gravel road, but it does a lot of switching around. Follow it five or six miles from the turnoff you've passed, keeping an eye to the north. The west ridge of Grayrock is descending; there are cliffs and very steep spots for much of the early part of this. At the appropriate distance you should notice a little timbered saddle. There are some old logging roads along here going north toward the ridge. Pick the one that seems to be approaching this saddle most directly. Some of the others may work, too.

The best one heads just about straight north toward the saddle. When I climbed this route, I could drive in a half mile before fallen timber stopped the car. Now most of these side logging

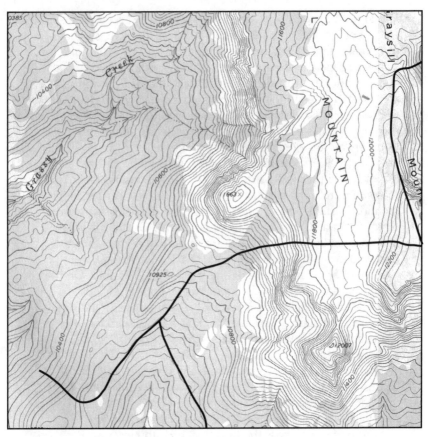

Graysill Mountain–Grayrock Peak

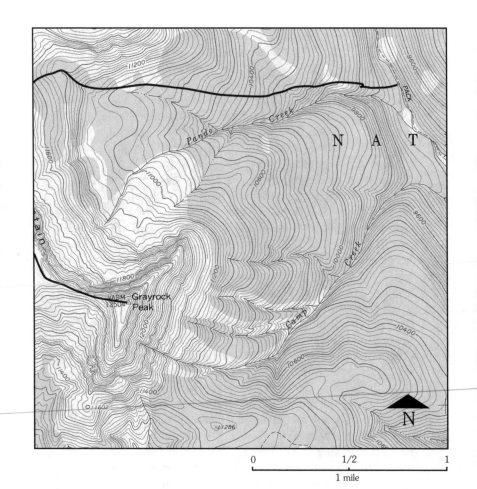

11200

10400

9600

PACK

Pando

Creek

N A T

9800

11600

11000

10600

tain

10000

Creek

11800

VABM Grayrock
12504 Peak

11200

11400

Camp

10400

1400

11400

10600

○11602

N

×11286

10600

0   1/2   1

1 mile

roads have been bulldozed shut at the main gravel road, but I think they could still be hiked profitably. It may be possible to locate the one I prefer. As you are rounding a curve heading northwest, there is a wide, clear spot on the right with parking space for a lot of cars. One of these old logging roads starts out from the far side of this area. It would take about a mile of fairly flat hiking to reach the base of the ridge below the desired saddle. If you miss this spot, you can continue on the gravel road through some more twists and turns about two miles farther. At this point, the talus rock from the west ridge of the mountain comes down through an opening in the trees all the way to the road. You can park here and start climbing up the talus, which does have a few trees mixed in with the rocks at first. Unfortunately, this route adds to both the length and the elevation gain. It would add an hour or more of time to the total hike—still a good climb but longer. If you go this route, climb east into the open and seek out the crest of the ridge to your left when you can. If you find the route to the saddle, turn right at the top of it. Both routes now proceed together to the east toward the summit of Grayrock. A pretty good trail leads through timber at first, then through an open meadow that rises gently to a rocky area. In one spot, the rocks form a fairly steep talus slope; above this, the going is easier again.

There is still more than a mile to go, but you are on top of the world and can see great distances in all directions because you are above timberline. At first, this section is quite wide. Your best bet is to stay somewhere near the middle as you continue eastward. After the steep talus, the route gradually narrows to just a few feet in width and drops off on both sides. The hiking is still easy. The rocks underfoot are small and noisy, sometimes with a musical sound and sometimes with just a clunk. One climber who had done quite well on the climb up to this point was so unnerved by the clinking and clunking that he was afraid to go the rest of the distance—now fairly short—to the top. The route widens out again at the finish—so much so that you might have trouble determining the actual high spot if it weren't for a big cairn located there.

The distance from my parking spot to the summit was about four miles, about half of it above timberline. The return is by the same route, unless you elect to leave a car at the approach by the Pando Creek route. It should be easy to find the way down that route, for at the top and just west of the top you can look almost straight down to the road. The west slope is very gradual; the east and north sides are nearly precipitous.

Hermosa Peak

Distance: *3.5 miles (round trip)*
Starting elevation: *11,520 feet*
Elevation gain: *1,059 feet*
High point: *12,579 feet*
Rating: *Moderate*
Time allowed: *1.5 to 2.5 hours*
Maps: *7.5′ Hermosa Peak; San Juan National Forest*

Hermosa Peak involves traveling some backcountry roads, but it is one of the easiest and quickest high-altitude climbs in southwestern Colorado. It offers fine views of even higher peaks from its top; even driving the road to it is a worthwhile experience. The climb is quite short but is rated moderate because it is high and because some 250 yards of it are steep, with one short hazardous spot.

Access is via the Bolam Pass four-wheel-drive road. This road, however, is usually in better condition than many such roads. Under dry conditions, two-wheel-drive cars and trucks can usually make it if they have good clearance and a good low gear for the steep hills. This road may be approached from the east or the west. For the eastern approach, take U.S. Highway 550 twenty-eight miles north of Durango to the Purgatory Ski Area turnoff; go north on it to the Purgatory parking area. At the east end of the parking lot, go north up a gravel road. This leads up above Purgatory and furnishes fine views of the ski runs, the valley below, and the West Needles–Twilight massif east across Lime Creek. This is especially spectacular during the fall foliage color season (the end of September and early October). At the top of the ridge above Purgatory this road turns north; four-tenths of a

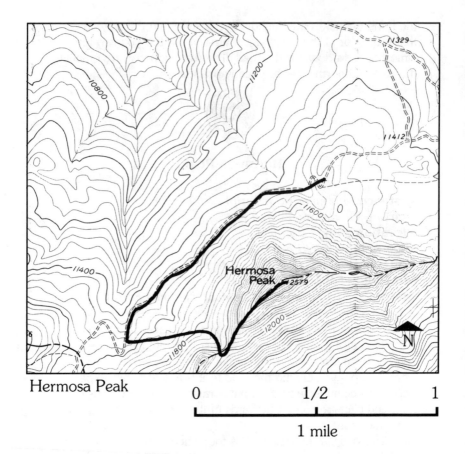

Hermosa Peak

0   1/2   1

1 mile

mile beyond this, take the first left down into Hermosa Park. This is a lovely valley surrounded by aspen- and spruce-covered mountains. At the west end of the park the road turns north and follows closely beside Hermosa Creek. This is a good-sized stream and must be forded a mile above the park. Except during the high water of spring snowmelt, the fording should be no problem even for two-wheel-drive cars if you approach it resolutely and do not try to cross too slowly.

Six miles beyond the ford and 1,900 feet higher you come to a little open shelf and the mining ghost town of Graysill. It is in better condition than some abandoned mining towns because it was involved in uranium and vanadium mining, putting it into a later period of history. It is worth a stop here for a view and a picture back down Hermosa Valley. One and four-tenths miles farther brings you to the top of Bolam Pass at 11,400 feet. Here again you get a good view. To the north and a little east is Grizzly Peak, just short of 14,000 feet. To the northwest, you look across Lizard Head Pass to Lizard Head Peak and the San Miguel massif, which contains three fourteeners: Wilson Peak, Mount Wilson, and El Diente.

Seven-tenths of a mile beyond Bolam Pass you make a sharp little dip down to cross over a culvert carrying a small stream. Just beyond this the main road turns right, but to go to Hermosa Peak, which dominates the southern skyline, turn left. This road starts southeast but soon turns southwest across an open, flat meadow. Follow the road to a large barrier; park here, cross the barrier, and hike on down the road about a mile. You will be following the Colorado Trail, which joins the route just beyond the barrier. The right place to leave the road-trail is a point just west of a saddle between Hermosa Peak and a smaller unnamed peak south of it.

It is eighteen miles from U.S. Highway 550 at the Purgatory turnoff to the point where the Hermosa Peak Road separates off from the Bolam Pass Road.

Access from the west route is via Colorado State Highway 145. On this side the road is called Barlow Creek Road, but it is the same road as Bolam Pass Road. It turns east off Highway 145 six miles north of Rico or six miles south of Lizard Head Pass. Just across the Dolores River a very nice forest service campground is located north of the road along the river. Barlow

Creek Road turns right, whereas the road straight ahead goes on into the campground. It is seven miles and 1,800 feet of rise on up to the route that turns off to Hermosa Peak. This junction is in an open space in a flat area, so it should not be hard to find. From there on, follow the directions given above to reach the peak.

The climb starts out east up an easy, grassy slope. (There may be a few trees at first, depending on your choice of where to start up.) The grassy slope heads toward the saddle, about a quarter-mile uphill. This is quite easy climbing except just below the saddle, where it gets steeper and becomes talus.

At the saddle, go left (northeast) toward the top a half-mile beyond. A hundred yards above the saddle there is one small cliff to get over, but most anyone can make it with care and a little boost from a companion. Once above this, it is a short but steep climb to the ridge; the top is a few hundred yards beyond.

Our hiking group climbed Hermosa Peak during the foliage color season a few years ago. We had along a guest from the Midwest who had come out to photograph the aspen. This was his first time on a mountain; with some encouragement he made the top with no difficulty, but on the steep part near the top he insisted on crawling on his hands and knees because he was so frightened of the height and steepness. There really was no serious risk; going down he was braver.

The top of the mountain does furnish some beautiful views. All the same mountains that you can see from Bolam Pass can be seen even better from here, plus more. There is a fine view of Engineer Mountain to the east. Blackhawk is the nearest to the southwest. The La Platas loom on the southern horizon.

The north face of Hermosa Peak is practically straight down. It can furnish its own kind of thrill if you look down.

The return should be made by the same route as the approach.

One of my trips here was on a lovely summer evening. My companion and I watched a beautiful sunset from the top as the red disk slipped behind the peaks west of us.

Hikes out of Silverton

South Mineral Creek–Cascade Valley

Distance: *8.8 miles (one way)*
Starting elevation: *10,680 feet*
Elevation gain: *1,800 feet*
High point: *12,480 feet*
Rating: *Moderate, but fairly long*
Time allowed: *5 to 7 hours*
Maps: *7.5' Ophir; 7.5' Engineer Mountain; San Juan National Forest*

This is a hike that is highly rewarding in beauty without requiring any difficult climbing. The beauty is in the natural scenery of nearby peaks and in a large expanse of wildflowers. Some people use this route for backpacking and an overnight stay, but it certainly can be done in a day, including time to enjoy the scenery and take pictures. It is a hike that does not return to the starting point; you will need someone to take you to the starting point and pick you up at the other end. A four-wheel-drive is best, but in dry weather a vehicle with good clearance can make it.

The launching point is South Mineral Campground. The road to the campground turns off U.S. Highway 550 two miles northwest of Silverton. It turns sharply downhill off the south side of the highway. Five miles down the road is the lovely campground in tall timber next to the stream, a very nice place to spend the night if you wish to start early the next morning. Four-wheel-drive and high-clearance vehicles can take hikers another two and one-half miles over a very rough road. (If you start hiking from the campground, you must add two and one-half miles and an hour to the distance and time given above.) The road goes west around the campground and turns southwest up a steep, rocky grade. It soon rises above timberline and continues on past the Bandora Mine one-half mile, where it stops at an old cabin.

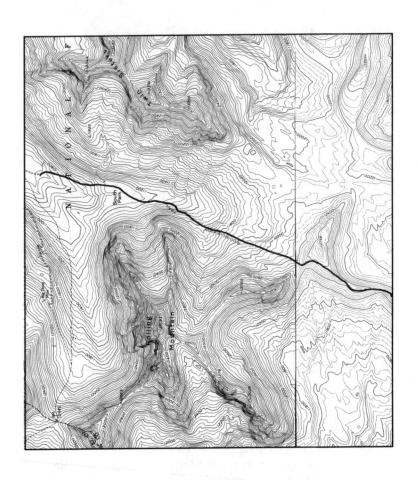

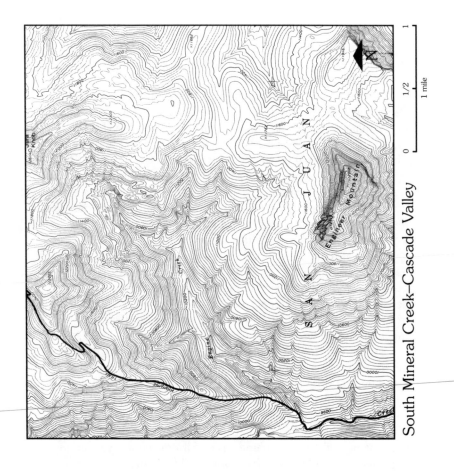

South Mineral Creek–Cascade Valley

The hike goes south from here, entering the forest for one-half mile before reaching and maintaining a higher level above the woods. This trail is called Rico-Silverton; farther along it becomes the Engine Creek Trail.

Above the timber you enter a nice level spot called South Park. Some of this is marshy. The wildflowers begin here with lovely marsh flowers and continue for a mile and a half up to the top of the basin at the pass, changing species with the altitude. This area can hardly be surpassed for natural floral beauty. But that is not all, for you pass Rolling Mountain (13,693 feet) on the right and the Twin Sisters (13,432 feet and 13,374 feet) steeply up on the left. At the top of the pass, an unnamed peak rises less than 300 feet above the trail. If you have plenty of time, it is worth a side trip up here to get a more complete view.

Near at hand to the southeast is Jura Knob. Several miles beyond that on the horizon are Twilight and the West Needles. Straight south is Engineer Mountain; from this side it is a dramatic cliff plunging 1,200 feet, not the graceful cone so often seen from the south side. To the southwest lies Grizzly, thrusting its rugged point skyward out of Cascade Valley's west side.

At the top of the pass you will cross the Colorado Trail coming up to the pass from the west and descending eastward. It may be more distinct than the path you are on; your trail goes south and follows a ridge just beyond the pass, whereas the Colorado Trail descends more rapidly to the west (on your right). It is a great trail but will not get you to your destination. At this point, your trail changes names: Rico-Silverton goes west and is the route of the Colorado Trail; your trail from here south is Engine Creek Trail.

South of the pass, you continue for another mile and a half above timberline. Here the trail becomes indistinct, but you should be able to get through this without much trouble if you contour around, generally south, toward a north-south saddle between the peak you have just climbed and the next one, also unnamed. Stay on the west side of the saddle and traverse the steep hillside, staying at about the same level. Around the south end of this peak you should pick up the trail again a little before it dips back into the timber.

Not far into the timber, the trail passes a nice spring with delicious drinking water. A short distance farther there is a narrow break in the trees at a little level spot. This presents a very powerful view across the deep Engine Creek Canyon of Engineer Mountain rising steeply, at first with beautiful timber and higher up into its rocky grandeur. The last time I was in this area, we camped overnight in the level spot; when the sun went down, the moon shone brightly over Engineer, completing the perfect picture. I thought, There is nowhere else in the world I would rather be right now.

Up to this point, the route has remained high; south beyond here, the trail descends rapidly—1,800 feet in 1.6 miles—to Cascade Creek and a little open flat where Engine Creek joins Cascade. This is a nice spot, good for relaxing and enjoying Cascade Creek as it works its way loudly through the rocks. You might even be able to catch a trout here.

Just a few yards upstream, the Highline Trail crosses the creek and heads west; instead of following it, pick up the Cascade Creek Trail and head downstream. In just a short distance you cross Engine Creek on a good forest service bridge. Just above the bridge, Engine Creek has a beautiful waterfall well worth exploring and photographing. In early June, before the snow has melted enough for this full hike, it is worth hiking up to the waterfall from the south end just to see the falls. Engine Creek at this time is a raging torrent pouring tons of water over the falls every minute.

There is a Cascade Creek road that leaves Highway 550 on the north side of its crossing of Cascade Creek. You could have your transportation come up this road one and a half miles to meet you; if this is done you will have a pleasant 2.4 miles more to hike down the trail from the falls. This is not steep; it leads along Cascade Creek, mostly in big timber, but with a few open spots and wildflowers. This is a lovely hike in its own right. There are several private cabins on the rest of the road down to the highway.

An alternative to the road is a new trail the forest service recently built to bypass the cabins. It swings around east uphill and in about a mile and a half comes out at a forest service guard station. A hundred yards before getting to the station road the trail joins the Engineer Mountain Trail in a right turn. Together they go another 100 yards south to the trailhead, ending 100 yards east of the station and 200 yards west of the highway. This location on the highway is a mile above the old road into the cabins at the Cascade Creek crossing.

Lake Hope

Distance: *5.3 miles (round trip)*
Starting elevation: *9,900 feet*
Elevation gain: *3,110 feet*
High point: *12,445 feet*
Rating: *Moderate*
Time allowed: *3 hours*
Maps: *7.5′ Ophir; Uncompahgre National Forest*

Lake Hope lies at the center of its own high basin a little above timberline. It is surrounded by dramatic sharp peaks well above 13,000 feet. There is a breathtaking ruggedness. Some of the peaks are very colorful, with a mixture of reds, oranges, and grays. The lake can at times provide good fishing. It is reachable by a well-maintained national forest trail. It is rated easy, though the last half-mile is a bit steep.

An interesting aspect of this lake is that it is a part of the water supply for the Ames power plant. Lake Hope is at the headwaters of the Lake Fork of the San Miguel River. Its water flows into Trout Lake. The varying demands of water for power can make Lake Hope beautiful when full and less attractive when drained down. This can also affect the fishing.

From Trout Lake, the water passes through a flume to the power plant. Ames is where the first commercial alternating current in the United States was generated. The motivation here was getting power more conveniently to the high-altitude mines in the area. It was difficult in the nineteenth century to get steam boilers and other heavy steam equipment up into this rugged high country. Another problem for the mine operators who used steam was fuel. Many mines were located well above timberline, so hauling wood for firing the boilers was an expensive uphill job. Some of the mines were in danger of being shut down because of this cost.

Direct-current electricity was no answer either because of the difficulty in transmitting it over anything but short distances. The pioneers hit upon the idea of alternating current for ease of transmission and low losses in power. Its voltage could be easily raised for long-distance transmission and again easily lowered for use. Building a power line over a mountain was much easier than hauling heavy equipment where roads were inadequate at best. There were many doubters, but the Ames plant was put into operation in 1892 and ran successfully for thirty days without a shutdown.

The route to Lake Hope from the west side is via Highway 145. Trout Lake is on the east side of the highway two miles north of Lizard Head Pass between Telluride and Rico. This is about twelve miles south of the Telluride turnoff from Highway 145. At Trout Lake there is a good gravel road along the north side of the lake. A signpost down the road a way indicates it is #626. Take it for one and two-thirds miles from the highway, then turn left uphill on route #627 for another two and one-half miles. This climbs steeply at times but is quite satisfactory for ordinary cars, at least when it is dry. At this point the road switches back sharply to the left but there is good parking here for several cars, and the trailhead is well marked. The trail is a good one. It climbs just over 1,000 feet to the lake in two and one-half miles; it goes on above the lake another half-mile, where it joins the route coming from the east side.

Lake Hope can also be approached from the east side. This is the route given on the map on the preceding page. For this route, go two miles northwest of Silverton on U.S. Highway 550, and turn left downhill on South Mineral Creek Road. The South Mineral Campground, a nice one, is located five miles down this road. A four-wheel-drive vehicle is recommended beyond the campground. Follow the road around the campground southwest about two and one-half miles to the Bandora Mine. There are interesting beaver ponds in the course of the creek both before and beyond the campground.

The Ophir quad map shows two trails up to Lake Hope through a canyon on the north side of Rolling Mountain. The lower one starts out bravely enough but soon dissipates in the woods. The other one, however, is a good trail; in fact, it is an old road nearly all the way to the top of the pass. The first part

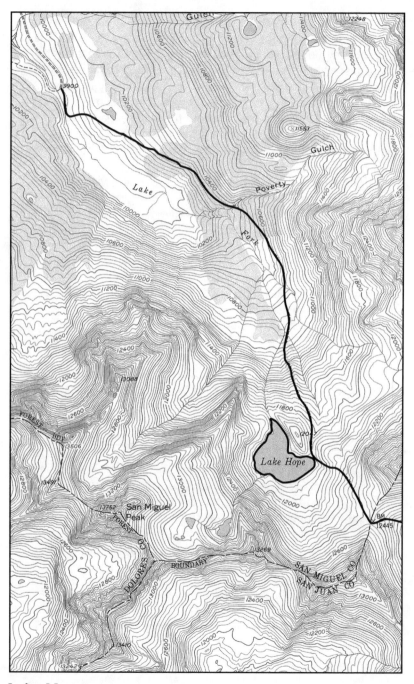

Lake Hope

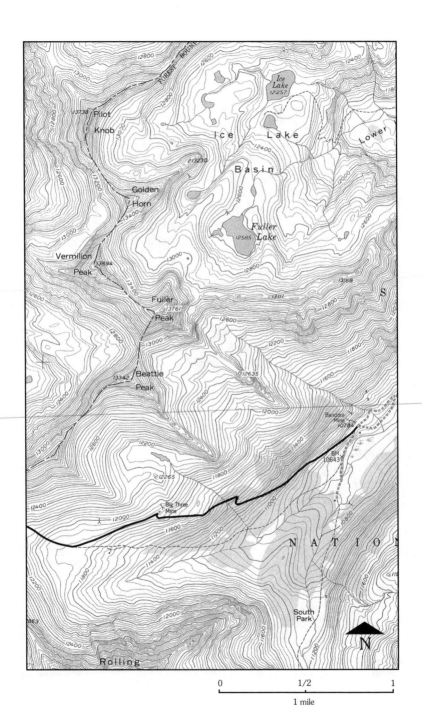

Ice Lake
12257

Ice   Lake

Lower

Pilot
Knob

13738

13230

B a s i n

Golden
Horn

13400

Fuller
Lake
12585

Vermilion
Peak

13894

13000

13768

13200

Fuller
Peak

13376

1311

13000

12635

Beattie
Peak

13342

Bandora
Mine
10784

BM
10643

12265

Big Three
Mine

N A T I O N

South
Park

Rolling

1863

N

0   1/2   1

1 mile

can be traveled by four-wheel-drive, but it is not worth it, for part of the road has slid away not far up.

The plan, then, is to park just below the Bandora Mine in the flat meadows off the road. Start hiking uphill on the old road on the southwest side of the mine. This route is not maintained and is rocky in places, but it is easy to follow and not too steep. It goes all the way to the top of the pass and then down the other side seven-tenths of a mile to the lake. The view at the top of the pass is dramatic as you first glimpse the sharp peaks, Lake Hope below, and Trout Lake still farther down.

This road is three miles long, one way. It starts at 10,784 feet at the mine, rises to 12,445 feet at the pass, and drops 565 feet to the lake at 11,880 feet. The total altitude gain one way, from the campground to the pass, is 2,545 feet; from the mine it is 1,661 feet. This route should be rated easy except for the four-wheel-drive approach and the high altitude, which changes it to moderate.

Ice Lakes

Distance: *7 miles (round trip)*
Starting elevation: *9,850 feet*
Elevation gain: *2,407 feet*
High point: *12,257 feet*
Rating: *Moderate*
Time allowed: *4 to 5 hours*
Maps: *7.5′Ophir; San Juan National Forest*

There are two Ice Lake basins—upper and lower. The upper (main) basin is far more interesting. The lower basin is on the way to the upper; its lake is small and shallow. The main basin lies above 12,000 feet and is one of the most interesting high-altitude basins in the San Juans. There are two rather large lakes (several acres each) and several small ones. Ice Lake is at 12,257 feet. Three-quarters of a mile south of it at 12,585 feet is Fuller

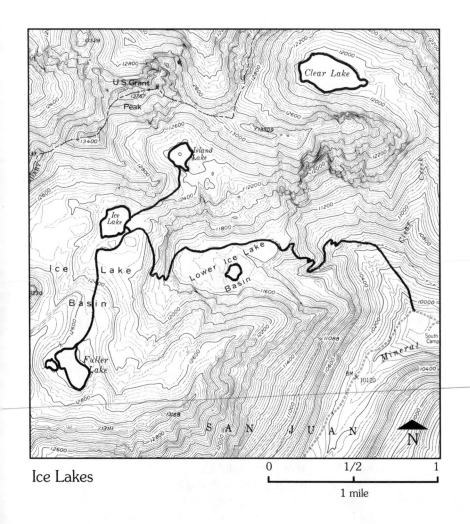

Ice Lakes

0   1/2   1

1 mile

Lake. About the same distance northeast of Ice Lake on a traverse around the end of a ridge in its own basin is Island Lake. This whole basin area is surrounded by sharp and colorful peaks, all well above 13,000 feet but none quite reaching 14,000 feet.

I will describe only the hike to the basin. The peaks all make interesting climbs, but climbers can find their own routes out of the basin rather easily, for this is all open country well above timberline. These peaks, in order from south around west to north, are: Fuller Peak (13,761 feet), Vermillion Peak (13,894 feet), Golden Horn (13,600 feet), Pilot Knob (13,738 feet), and U.S. Grant Peak (13,767 feet). Clear Lake, even larger than those named, is only a mile northeast of Island Lake and at a slightly lower altitude, but a high ridge separates it off. Therefore, it is to be approached by a different route.

To get to the trailhead for Ice Lakes, take U.S. Highway 550 two miles northwest of Silverton. Make a left turn downhill into the valley and drive six miles to the lovely South Mineral Campground. Park here; hike on up the road to the point where it turns south and crosses a stream. Just a few yards before this point, the Ice Lakes Trail climbs right, steeply up the hill (north and west). Later it moves more westerly, climbing steadily through both straight stretches and switchbacks up to the lower basin. The trail does not climb much through the lower basin; in fact, it descends a bit. At the far end of the basin it begins to climb again; the first 200 yards are rocky and furnish the only difficulty in the whole trail, but it is bad in only one short spot. Another mile brings you to beautiful Ice Lake.

This is an easy trail to follow into the large upper basin, where it quits; then you are on your own to explore the lakes and the surrounding guardian peaks. You cannot see out except to the east through South Mineral Creek Valley. But the surrounding peaks and the lakes make the hike well worthwhile. These lakes are high but large enough for good fishing. There are many beautiful wildflowers along the route and small tundra flowers in the basin itself.

The return is to be made by the same route as the approach.

Climbing above Island Lake toward the saddle on the southeast side of Ulysses S. Grant Peak.

Island Lake

A short and worthwhile extension of the Ice Lake trip is Island Lake. Fuller Lake is in the same basin as Ice Lake, but Island Lake is separated off in its own basin and needs some additional explanation. It is six-tenths of a mile farther and, at 12,400 feet, is 143 feet higher than Ice Lake. It is located in a tight glacial pocket surrounded by U.S. Grant Peak and its shoulder ridges. There is a single large flat-topped rock island rising out of the middle of it.

To get to Island Lake, hike northeast, starting on the north side of the stream that drains Ice Lake. At first there is no trail, but looking ahead a little in the tundra you can see several sheep trails converging. From this point on there is a well-defined trail the rest of the way around an east-west ridge to the lake. The trail has a couple of rocky spots, but the hike can be completed easily in twenty minutes. Ice Lake is frequented by many on nice weekend summer days, but Island Lake is more isolated and is seen by a much smaller number of people. It is beautiful and well worth the extra time.

Ascending the steep, small ledges of U.S. Grant above the saddle.

U.S. Grant Peak

Those who wish to consider climbing U.S. Grant Peak will want to come around to Island Lake and climb along its south side to a saddle between Grant and an unnamed peak to the south. At the saddle, turn right up the ridge. It has a few difficult spots, the most difficult being where it joins the main part of the mountain. Here is a straight-up spot about five feet high, but the holds are adequate for you to make it up. At the top is a narrow ledge. The ledge appears to be blocked off, but a close squeeze next to it, going right around the corner, opens up to easier going and a scramble up to the summit. All the tops in this area are very rugged. Grant rises 1,367 feet above the lake.

Clear Lake

Distance: *7.5 miles (round trip)*
Starting elevation: *9,850 feet*
Elevation gain: *2,110 feet*
High point: *11,960 feet*
Rating: *Moderate*
Time allowed: *4.5 to 5.5 hours*
Maps: *7.5'Ophir; San Juan National Forest*

Clear Lake also lies above South Mineral Campground in a high-walled, tightly shaped glacial cirque. The peaks rise abruptly to over 13,000 feet right out of the lake on two sides. The north and east sides leave enough room for camping and picnicking, but the total effect on the hiker is that of being in a big, rocky pocket.

The lake itself is four-tenths of a mile long and about half that wide. It is a good fishing spot but, being well above timberline, its surroundings show a harsh and rugged beauty.

There is currently an active mine high on the talus above the south side of the lake. Because of the mine, you can drive all the way to the lake on a well-maintained four-wheel-drive road, which is good enough for two-wheel-drive vehicles with high clearance when it is dry.

For hiking, you can go all the way on the road beginning two-thirds of a mile down the road toward the highway from South Mineral Campground. A more interesting route for hiking starts at the northwest corner of the campground. The Ice Lake and Clear Lake trails are one and the same for seven-tenths of a mile, where the Ice Lake Trail switches back left. The Clear Lake Trail goes straight on, crossing Clear Creek at a very nice falls. A couple hundred yards farther, the trail joins the road and uses it the rest of the way to the top, two and three-fourths miles.

South Mineral Creek Valley is surrounded by steep walls and rugged, jagged peaks. Many breathtaking views appear along this route; it is well worth hiking in spite of the road.

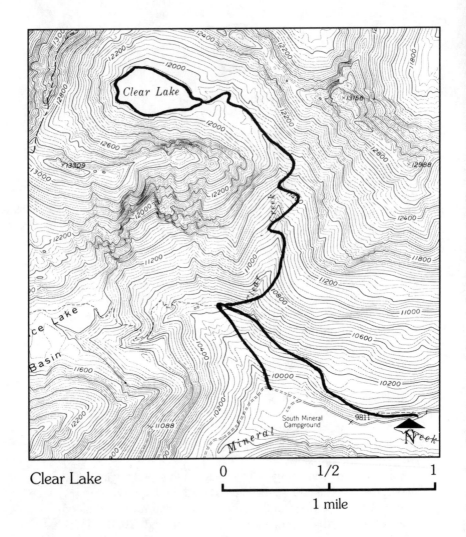

Clear Lake

Kendall Mountain

Distance: *12 miles (round trip)*
Starting elevation: *9,300 feet*
Elevation gain: *3,766 feet*
High point: *13,066 feet*
Rating: *Moderate*
Time allowed: *6 to 7 hours*
Maps: *7.5' Silverton; San Juan National Forest*

Kendall Mountain is just over 13,000 feet and is located directly east of Silverton. The hike described here is up a steep rocky road. Four-wheel-drive vehicles can go most of the way to the top. Two-wheel-drives can go halfway or more so that the total length of the hike can be reduced substantially if you choose to do so.

Kendall Mountain, over this same route, is the site of an annual footrace each summer. If you hike it, you will see that it has to be grueling for a race. The best runners make the round trip in under two hours.

The main street in Silverton is Greene Street. Three blocks north of the south end of it, turn right and follow this street to a bridge across the Animas River. Park on either side of the bridge in a convenient spot and start hiking south along the base of the mountain. The road spirals around and up the mountain, at first south, then southeast, east, and finally north to the top. Most of the route is open so that many fine views are accessible along most of the way. At four miles, turn left (north) toward the peak. The main road goes on up Kendall Gulch to several old mines. Near the top the road quits, and you have to finish the climb over talus; it is only a few hundred yards.

The return should be over the same route.

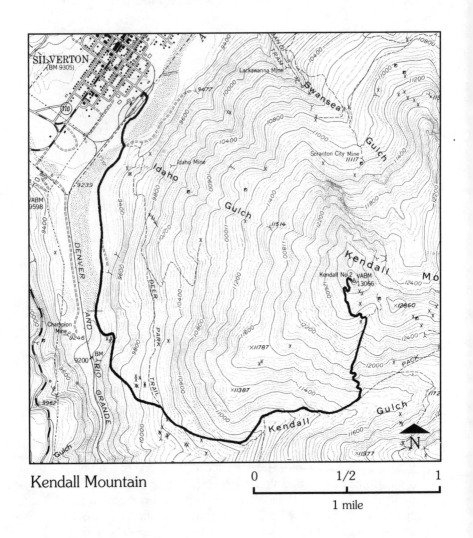

Kendall Mountain

0   1/2   1

1 mile

Kendall Mountain from the north end of Silverton.

Deer Park Trail–Whitehead Peak

Distance: *13.2 miles (round trip)*
Starting elevation: *9,300 feet*
Elevation gain: *3,959 feet*
High point: *13,259 feet*
Rating: *Difficult (due to length and altitude)*
Time allowed: *6 to 8 hours*
Maps: *7.5' Silverton; 7.5' Howardsville; San Juan National Forest*

This hike includes a lovely high-altitude basin at timberline and a peak with good views. It lies southeast of Silverton off the Kendall Mountain Road. (See the Kendall Mountain hike on how to start up this road.) The hike distance and elevation gain are calculated from the bridge over the Animas River at Silverton.

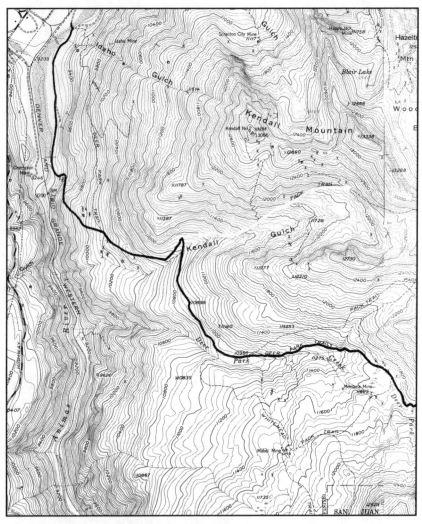

Deer Park Trail–Whitehead Peak

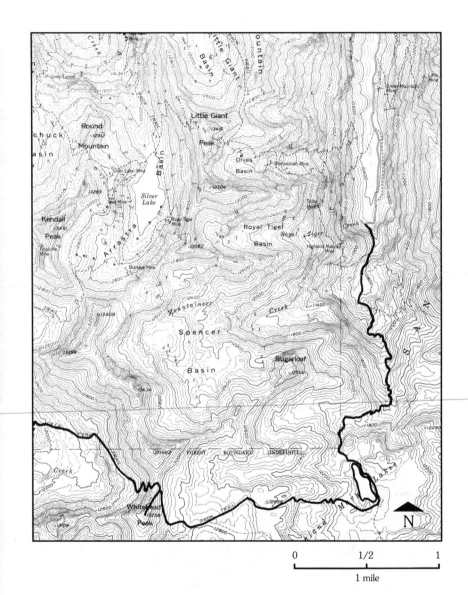

0   1/2   1

1 mile

This can be shortened a great deal by those who want to drive partway. Four-wheel-drive vehicles can go all the way to the basin, cutting the round-trip hike by 6.3 miles and 1,620 feet of elevation. Two-wheel-drives can cut off four or more miles.

To start the hike, take the Kendall Mountain road up 2.3 miles from the river bridge to a right turn on a smaller road; it is an easy, pleasant mile beyond this to the Deer Park basin.

At the head of the basin (east) is a saddle between two high points. The one on the right is Whitehead Peak. In the basin there are several trails. To climb Whitehead, aim for the saddle, but start out at the lower end of the basin, following a little jeep road on the left (north) side that runs along the flat near the stream for most of a mile before climbing left uphill to a little plateau. The trail can be lost easily at the turnoff, for the road leads across the stream to an old cabin on the south side of the basin. The correct trail stays on the north side; from the plateau, it moves east and eventually southeast, then mounts the steep part to the top of the saddle through a series of switchbacks. Some of the trail is faint in this area. Whitehead Peak is a large rolling top a few hundred yards to the south of the saddle.

From the top there is a good view south to the Grenadiers. The view to the east down across the tundra includes the Highland Mary Lakes. In fact, the trail leads on across the saddle down to these lakes in open tundra in just over two miles. You could go there and north down the Highland Mary Trail to the head of Cunningham Gulch as an alternate way out, assuming you have a way of being picked up there. From the saddle next to Whitehead to Cunningham via the lakes is five miles, all down-hill. (See the Highland Mary Lakes hike for details of that route.)

The return can be made by the approach route. The 13.2-mile round trip in the heading is based on this.

There is still another route. It swings south, then west around the base of Whitehead and back to Deer Park Trail. It is 1.8 miles farther but is a more gradual trail. (Some might choose to follow it for the approach also.) To take it, follow the trail down the east side of the saddle as if going to Highland Mary Lakes. It starts south and a little east, then swings east. In a half-mile, the trail divides; straight ahead goes to the lakes. A right turn takes you southwest along the base of the peak. In six-tenths of a mile you come to the Whitehead Trail. Take a right turn on it, and go west along the rim of Whitehead Gulch. After a mile, the trail swings northwest across Whitehead Mesa and in two miles comes back to the west end of Deer Park Basin; from here on, the route is the same as the approach. This route passes through a small strip of private property and mining areas.

Highland Mary Lakes

Distance: *6 miles (round trip)*
Starting elevation: *10,400 feet*
Elevation gain: *1,650 feet*
High point: *12,090 feet*
Rating: *Moderate to difficult*
Time allowed: *3 to 5 hours*
Maps: *7.5'Howardsville; San Juan National Forest*

Highland Mary Lakes is a favorite high-altitude area for fishing and for just being around water above timberline. The area has one large lake and several smaller ones. They are in a big tundra basin with a number of peaks visible around them.

To reach the lakes, go to the north end of Greene Street (the main street in Silverton) and turn right on Colorado State Route 110; follow this road four and one-fourth miles northeast to a right turn up Cunningham Gulch. Follow this road southeast four miles to its end at the head of the canyon. Along this route other roads turn off up the mountainside, but the main road stays near the bottom of the canyon near Cunningham Creek.

Some hikers stop here and park off to the side, but you can go on profitably for two-thirds mile. The road crosses a bridge that does not inspire much confidence. Go west, curving to the north and then turn back to the south, climbing a hill above the bridge and a rapids area in the creek. The road then curves right and goes uphill. Before long, you come to a sharp turnoff that goes steeply down to the left. Take this road down to the creek, where it must be forded. If you park the car before the bridge,

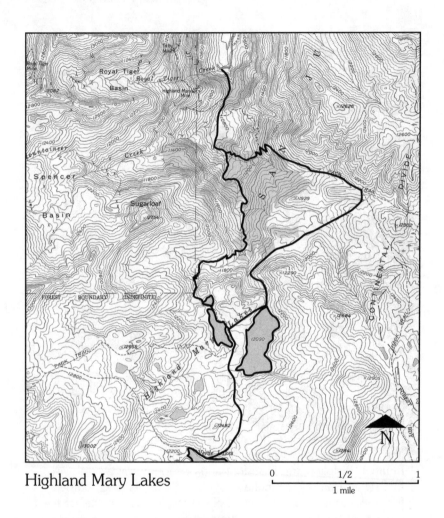

Highland Mary Lakes

you will have to wade the creek here. Once across it, you can drive on south for another 300 yards, where you must park in a good grassy area. The trail becomes singletrack here and enters the woods. It follows the creek on the east side for a mile and then crosses it. There usually is a pretty good log to use here. The stream is narrower here than the fording spot below. After this crossing, you will be going west uphill, reaching timberline quickly. It twists around quite a bit, then bears to the south, going uphill steeply. Soon you arrive at the first lake, on your right. A little farther ahead you come to the largest lake, on your left.

The Verde Lakes are also worth visiting and lie one-half mile south of the southwest corner of the largest of the Highland Mary Lakes. There is a trail, but the Verde Lakes are easy to find anyway, since all this territory is open tundra above timberline. The Verde Lakes are only 100 feet higher. A quarter-mile south of Verde Lakes and a half-mile west is still another accessible lake called Lost Lake. It is at about the same altitude.

The return from this hike is by the approach route. However, another option is to go west along a trail from the Highland Marys two miles over Whitehead Peak and back into Silverton via Deer Park Trail, as described on page 197.

Highland Mary Lakes can also be approached from another route via Spencer Basin. For this one, go to the head of Cunningham Gulch as before, but follow an old mining road west up out of the gulch. Four-wheel-drive vehicles can make this road up into Spencer Basin about two miles up a series of switchbacks and across Mountaineer Creek to the south side of the basin. Out of the basin, hike south up 400 feet to a saddle. Over the saddle a little way you can look eastward down on the Highland Mary Lakes. It is just over a one-mile hike to them; most of the way there is no trail, but this offers no problem except for short patches of brush.

Back at the Highland Mary Lakes there is another route for returning. Go around the north end of the biggest lake and hike uphill to the northeast around the end of a ridge, about 500 feet above the lake. Turning more to the east after rounding the end of the hill, you soon cross another higher stream and then come to a north-south trail running along the top of the Continental Divide. In this area, the steepness gives way to smaller undulating hills—all above timberline. I was in this area in July one year, and at that time it was one vast flower garden as far as the eye could see.

To continue the journey back, follow the Divide Trail to the left; the Divide Trail will descend gently to an intersection with another trail. Take this one to the left; it descends more rapidly now and will bring you back to Cunningham Creek, close to your parking spot. Shortly before you get all the way down to complete the hike, the trail splits. Both routes go down to the creek, but the left one should be closer to where you want to be.

Continental Divide

Distance: *15 miles (round trip)*
Starting elevation: *10,450 feet*
Elevation gain: *2,390 feet*
High point: *12,840 feet*
Rating: *Difficult*
Time allowed: *10 to 13 hours*
Maps: *7.5′ Howardsville; 7.5′ Storm King; San Juan National Forest*

This is rather ambitious for a one-day hike, but strong hikers can make it all right. The trip is well worthwhile, for it is one of the highest and most beautiful hikes in the state of Colorado. The Continental Divide raises its spiny back across the entire width of the state north to south; there are trails along it in several places. This particular chunk is east of Silverton, where much of the best in the San Juan Mountains can be seen. Fortunately, most of the ascent is made in the first three miles. After that, it rises only gradually for the most part.

For this hike, go back to the parking place just described above at the end of the description of the Highland Mary Lakes hike. Follow this trail left (southeast) up to the Continental Divide Trail and turn right.

Elk portrait.

The projected hike goes five miles south on the Divide. At three and one-half miles the trail splits. The right side starts west and soon swings south and descends several hundred feet, joining the Elk Creek Trail, which heads west toward the Animas River. At the juncture of these trails Eldorado Lake lies directly south less than a half-mile, but there is a 400-foot cliff in between. Incidentally, the Colorado Trail follows the Elk Creek Trail at this point, ascending to the Divide. Because of the cliff you should take the left branch of the trail where it splits. This moves east a quarter of a mile, gently rising, then swings south. Soon you will join the Colorado Trail; it swings off to the left and down the east side of the Divide. Do not take this, but continue on south; this will be the Colorado Trail for a quarter of a mile until you reach the point where it is coming up from the west. You should keep going south for another quarter-mile to where a small trail goes right to Eldorado Lake, 300 feet below, in about a half-mile. The lake is at 12,504 feet.

This is a long hike and beautiful all the way, but the hiker can shorten it to just before Eldorado Lake.

Along the Continental Divide, the east side looks down into the headwaters of the Rio Grande River and into the Rio Grande

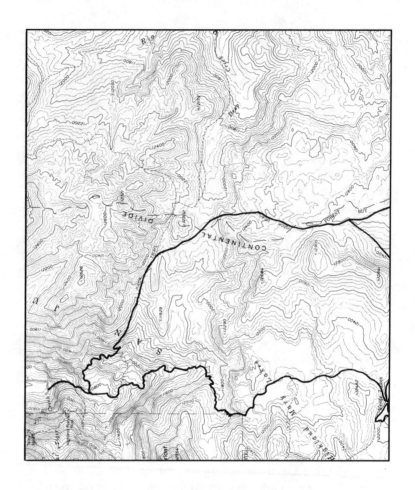

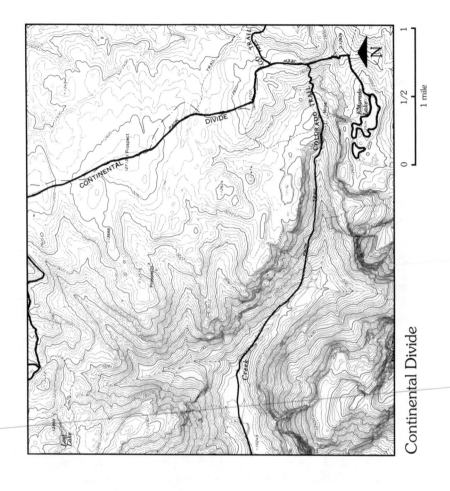

Continental Divide

National Forest. The west side looks into the Highland Mary Lakes Basin and, near the end of the hike, into the deep Elk Creek Canyon. But the most dramatic scenery is to the south and southwest, where rise the Grenadiers with many sharp and jagged peaks, their sheer cliffs plunging straight down along the north sides. Beyond the Grenadiers are the Needles. This is truly wild country!

The return trip can be made by the same route, but some of it can be varied. For this, go back along the same route about four miles, where there is a trail going west one and one-half miles to Verde Lakes. The start of this trail is not always obvious because it starts out over grass, which may or may not be worn down. There should, however, be a cairn at the right point; also, looking southwest from the right point you have one of the best views down through the beginning of a canyon to the Grenadier Range of stunning sharp peaks, some of the best in the San Juans. Start out southwest toward this canyon; the trail should become more distinct in a few hundred yards and be all right the rest of the way to the lakes. The trail actually enters the upper end of the canyon and then swings around a point out of it, soon heading quite westerly. From these lakes you can follow another trail north two-thirds of a mile to Highland Mary Lakes and pick up the trail that goes on down between the two largest lakes. Follow it three miles as it winds around, sometimes steeply, generally going north, back to your parking spot at the head of Cunning-ham Gulch.

If you might be interested in backpacking, you could spend the night at Eldorado Lake and then go back to the Colorado Trail, taking it west down Elk Creek to the Animas River and then out the Molas Trail to U.S. Highway 550. For this kind of hike one might want to spend a second night at or near the river, because the hike out involves a steep climb of close to 2,000 feet—on a very good trail, however. The Colorado Trail follows all of this route, until about a half-mile from the highway it splits, with the left branch (Colorado Trail) ascending to the top of Molas Pass at the highway, and the right branch going up to the parking spot just east of the highway about two-thirds of a mile north of the pass. It is hoped you have a second car waiting for you here.

Silver Lake

Distance: *2.5 miles (round trip)*
Starting elevation: *11,200 feet*
Elevation gain: *986 feet*
High point: *12,186 feet*
Rating: *Moderate*
Time allowed: *2 to 4 hours*
Maps: *7.5' Howardsville; San Juan National Forest*

Silver Lake is surrounded by many old mines. It is not good for fishing because the water is highly mineralized from the mines, but it is a great place for mining buffs and bottle hunters.

To get to Silver Lake, take Colorado State Road 110 northeast out of Silverton two miles to a right turn downhill and across the Animas River. This brings you into Arrastra Gulch. It is 2.8 miles up this road to the parking place at the Mayflower Mine. There are several side roads where you can get lost. At the first split, take the left fork, which takes you up the side of the canyon a little way and across the remains of an aerial tramway. Then the road turns right and parallels the tram above it for a half-mile. Another road turns left in the middle of the half-mile. Skip this one—it goes up to Little Giant Basin. The correct road continues paralleling the tramway and eventually crosses back to the right side of it. Then comes a switchback left and up. Two-wheel-drive vehicles should park here. This is above timberline. The fairly elaborate buildings of the Mayflower Mine are visible high above on the east side of the canyon. Hiking from here up the road to the mine adds a half-mile of distance and 600 feet of vertical gain. If the mine is being worked, all vehicles must park at the lower switchback.

From the mine, a good trail leads south and a little east on up to the lake in a mile and a quarter, some of which is fairly steep.

There is no road up to the lake and never has been. However, quite an operation took place there. Several buildings

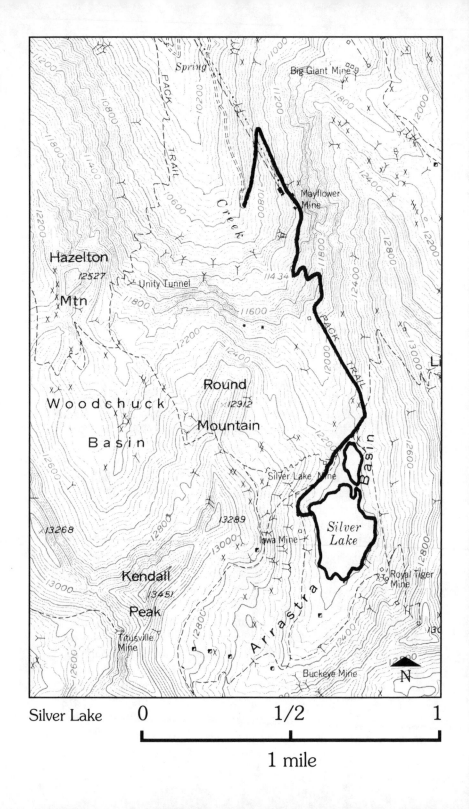

Silver Lake   0   1/2   1

1 mile

The Mayflower Mine on the steep mountainside on the approach to Silver Lake.

Snow tunnel.

were constructed for mining and milling the ore. By milling it there only the concentrate had to be carried down—over the steep trail—on the backs of mules. A few of the buildings are still in fairly good shape, although most have collapsed under the heavy snow, spilling their load of machinery. As a result, rollers and other equipment have mixed in with piles of building materials and a few old shoes, clothes, bed springs, and other junk. It is interesting to study the heaps to try to understand the way of life and work of these miners. The lake and the buildings are above timberline but are surrounded by still higher peaks except on the north side—your ascent route. The area is very isolated from the rest of civilization. There are no views out of this pocket.

There is another interesting thing about this hike. The picture shows the Mayflower Mine and the steepness of the mountainside. The trail traverses upward to the lake along this steep area. Partway up above the mine (shown in the picture) you come to an avalanche path that runs most winters, leaving a lot of snow along the way. If you are there before it all melts, you have a problem. The snow is likely to be quite firm. Making adequate and safe steps through it is difficult. If the steps are not deep enough, you are apt to be given a fast and dangerous trip to the bottom. The last group I took there faced this problem, but we found an interesting and safe solution. Where the snow goes over the trail, there is some vertical, solid rock on the uphill side. When warm weather arrives, the rocks warm up faster than the snow. When we came to this point, we found that the warm rocks had melted a tunnel under the deep part of the snow next to the rocks. We therefore hiked through a snow tunnel for about ten yards and came out safely on the other side, ready to complete the climb.

The return from this hike is by the same route as the ascent.

Tired but happy campers waiting for the Durango train at Needleton after climbing fourteeners around Chicago Basin, northeast of Durango.

The train arriving at Needleton.

The Area Fourteeners

Most people with some experience climbing in Colorado sooner or later get bitten by the "fourteener" bug. All of the highest mountains in Colorado are in this class. There are fifty-four mountains in the state above 14,000 feet. They start with Sunshine Peak at 14,001 feet and go to Mount Elbert at 14,433 feet, the highest in the state. Only Mount Whitney in California, of the other peaks in the contiguous states, is taller—and that is only by sixty-five feet. Geologically, the 14,000-foot bracket is the natural roof of the state.

These peaks present a unique challenge to the Colorado hiker; some of them are very difficult and are only for the thoroughly experienced climber. Others are not difficult at all; they are no more difficult than some lower climbs except that they present the problem of thin air. People with a history of heart trouble or high blood pressure should not attempt any of them without prior medical approval. For anyone else, a period of a few days of acclimatization at altitudes above 6,000 feet will be helpful. A person who has done some aerobic training, such as jogging or vigorous hiking at low altitude, will likely be all right. Everyone at these higher levels experiences some shortness of breath. For the well-trained, it only means slowing down some and taking frequent short rests. Older people in good physical shape are not to be discouraged. I have climbed a number of these high peaks with some group members who were at or near retirement age. These people when in good condition typically do well.

Twelve of the fifty-four fourteeners are located in southwest Colorado, the territorial limits of this book. They are: Handies, Redcloud, Sunshine, Wilson Peak, Mount Wilson, El Diente, Sunlight, Windom, Eolus, Sneffels, Wetterhorn, and Uncompahgre. I will describe the six of these that fit into the other limits set for this work: no technical climbing and no overnight backpacking. The other six involve more difficulty in climbing or overnight stays on the trail. Of the six described, some hikers may prefer to car-camp for a night if they have had to drive some distance to the trailhead, but none require the extra weight of sleeping equipment to be carried on the trail; day packs and canteens are adequate.

Climbers on Sunlight.

For those who want to branch out into other fourteeners anywhere in the state, I recommend two guidebooks for your consideration. The first is by The Colorado Mountain Club with Robert M. Ormes: *Guide to the Colorado Mountains,* fully revised ninth edition (1992), edited by Randy Jacobs, published by The Colorado Mountain Club. The second book is by Walter R. Borneman and Lyndon J. Lampert: *A Climbing Guide to Colorado's Fourteeners,* second edition (1990), published by Pruett Publishing Company.

One other caution needs to be given for fourteeners: the snow problem. Unless you enjoy snow climbing and like to use crampons and ice axes, climbing in these mountains should be restricted to July through early September. Some years, snow conditions permit a little earlier and/or a little later climb. Even during the prime time, you may be called upon to cross some small snowfields. This requires extra care if they are steep. The extra care means kicking good solid steps or using an ice axe if the snow is too hard for steps. If you don't have an ice axe, you may be able to go around the snow above or below.

Mount Sneffels

Distance: *3 miles (round trip)*
Starting elevation: *12,400 feet*
Elevation gain: *1,750 feet*
High point: *14,150 feet*
Rating: *Moderate*
Time allowed: *3 to 4 hours*
Maps: *7.5'Mt. Sneffels; 7.5'Telluride; Uncompahgre National Forest*

This is a fourteener but is fairly easy to climb by the route described below. The north face, however, is a challenge even for technical climbers. Since it is the highest point in the area, it commands tremendous views. I have found it especially rewarding in late September (if the snows have held off) during the season of aspen foliage color. The north and west sides of the mountain and the lower country to the south are mottled with gold mixed with the dark green of the high-altitude conifers. There is a long, wide valley to the north toward Ridgway and Montrose, with Grand Mesa in the dim distance. Immediately to the south is St. Sophia Ridge, containing a half-dozen or more peaks above 13,000 feet. Beyond that is lower timbered land, and still farther are the San Miguels, with three fourteeners, and the unique shaft pointing skyward known as Lizard Head. The fourteeners here are Mount Wilson, Wilson Peak, and El Diente. East are the many, many high peaks of the San Juans.

The mileage and altitude gain given above depend upon four-wheel-drive transportation. Two-wheel-drives will usually have to stop two miles and 1,600 feet farther down. The hiking in these two miles is easy on the road.

To reach Sneffels, go to Ouray on U.S. Highway 550, seventy-five miles north of Durango and thirty-seven miles south of Montrose. The highway itself between Durango and Ouray is one of the most scenic in the state. It is called "the million-dollar

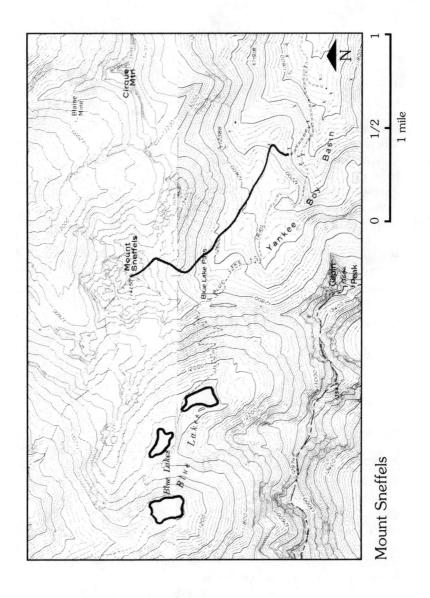

Mount Sneffels

Falls on Sneffels Creek in Yankee Boy Basin, below the climbing area.

highway" because of the gold ore in its base. It takes you over three passes that are 10,000 to 11,000 feet high. Sometimes you are riding on the edge of a sheer canyon wall. The twenty-five miles between Silverton and Ouray are some of the most avalanche-prone stretches of highway in Colorado. Many avalanche paths run regularly each winter. Most have names. Riverside is a real killer, having snuffed out five lives in the last fifteen years. There is an institute in Silverton for avalanche study. Much is yet to be known about what causes them to run at certain times and not at others. When they do run, they have tremendous force. Riverside falls several thousand feet; in recent years it has swept off the road and demolished both a bulldozer and a heavy snowplow truck, taking their operators to death in the process. Its fury was tamed in the summer of 1986, when the highway department built a snow shed over the road to take the sliding snow harmlessly across to the canyon below. The avalanche paths can be recognized in the summer by the treeless strips down a mountain that are surrounded on either side by heavy timber. Early in the summer there will be large hard piles of snow, often containing tree branches, at the bottoms of these chutes.

A well-deserved lunch break on top of Mount Sneffels.

Ouray is a picturesque little town nestled in a small valley with high cliffs rising all around it. The town calls itself "The Switzerland of America." To go to Sneffels from Ouray, take the Camp Bird Mine road. It turns off U.S. Highway 550 just after the first switchback at the south end of town as the highway begins to rise. This is a good gravel road going southwest to the Camp Bird entrance. Here it curves around west and eventually northwest into Yankee Boy Basin. In a flat spot is the ghost town of Sneffels, with the ruins of its large ore-processing mill. Most buildings are down. Winters in the high country soon collapse unoccupied buildings due to the very heavy snow load.

Yankee Boy Basin is a beautiful valley with many wildflowers and a lovely waterfall.

Beyond Camp Bird the road begins to get rough, and two-wheel-drives have to stop soon. After a fairly level spot just above timberline, the road climbs very steeply and ends up moving north on the north side of the basin. There is adequate parking here, but you should not move out onto the tundra with a vehicle because the tundra is very fragile and scars can last many years.

From the parking place, hike west across talus through a relatively flat area for three-quarters of a mile. There is a fairly good trail most of this way, which speeds up talus walking. At this point, you will come to a wide couloir or chute. Follow it north up a steep slope to a saddle. This will be fairly difficult climbing, because the scree on the slope makes you slip regularly. Often it is easier to step out of the main path and climb on rocks that are a little larger. The scree is great for a rapid, shuffling descent. At the saddle, turn west (left), and ascend another steep couloir; this one is filled with big rocks that you have to climb over and around. Just below the top of this, climb out the south side and on up the cone to the summit. There is a fairly well-worn route that you can follow easily. There is some exposure here, but it is not really dangerous if you move with care. The top is very small and can only accommodate a few people at a time. The wind is usually calm on this peak; you can enjoy the views and relax in comfort after the steep climb.

The descent is made by the same route as the climb. The scree becomes fun on the way down.

On the south side of the mountain is a small north-south ridge substantially below the summit separating Yankee Boy Basin from the Blue Lakes area. I feel confident you could return by this way if you wish to vary the route, but I have not tried it. If you park where I have suggested for four-wheel-drives, it would lengthen the return and involve some ascent back to your car. There is a trail in this area that leads back down the basin.

Wilson Peak

Distance: *8 miles (round trip)*
Starting elevation: *10,500 feet*
Elevation gain: *3,517 feet*
High point: *14,017 feet*
Rating: *Difficult*
Time allowed: *5 to 6 hours*
Maps: *7.5' Dolores Peak; 7.5' Mount Wilson; Uncompahgre National Forest*

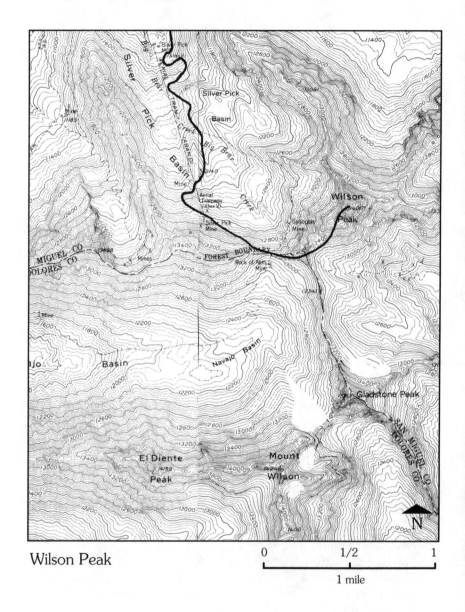

Wilson Peak

0   1/2   1

1 mile

Wilson Peak is one of three fourteeners in the San Miguel Mountains; as fourteener climbs go, it is not among the easiest but is easier than average. The other two in the group are Mount Wilson and El Diente ("the tooth" in Spanish); these two are much too difficult to fit into the scope of this guide. Both are quite hard at the top, and the ridge between them is known as one of the toughest in the state. But Wilson Peak can be climbed by anyone of durability and some rock-scrambling experience.

This is an area that has had a great deal of mining activity in the past, and some is going on now.

I will describe the Silver Pick route. This is not the only route, but is the shortest.

The approach is made from Highway 145 between Placerville and Telluride. About seven miles southeast of the Placerville junction of Highways 62 and 145 are the remnants of the town of Vanadium. A dirt road turns south off the highway here, crosses the San Miguel River, and follows up Bear Creek. (Don't make the mistake of turning off farther west at the Fall Creek turnoff.)

On the Bear Creek Road there are some possible turnoff roads; generally speaking, choose straight ahead at these options. Currently there are signs; choose those marked for Silver Pick. The distance from the highway to the Wilson Mountains Primitive Area barrier is about seven and one-half miles. There is a good parking and small camping area to the left of the road just before the barrier. Park or car-camp here. The last three to four miles of road are all right when dry for two-wheel-drives but require four-wheel-drives when wet. The rest of the road is good gravel.

Hiking starts up the same road beyond the barrier. At about a mile and a quarter, an old mill appears on the right with one building in rather good condition. Just before the building, the main road switches back left; follow it. After the next switchback, go about another quarter-mile to where the trail starts up steeply. It is small and easily missed, but once on it, you will find it un-mistakable. You could follow the road, but it is much longer and less interesting.

After climbing about 500 feet, you will be over the first hump of rocks and will be able to see the top of Wilson Peak, straight ahead. To the right of it is a saddle at 13,000 feet. A lit-tle farther on the trail divides, the left side going straight for the peak. The last 1,000 feet this way climb a steep couloir directly below the peak, which can be quite hazardous for the novice. The right fork of this trail is easier. It winds its way up to the saddle. On the way up on a little plateau are the remains of the old "hotel," a remarkably well-built stone structure where miners could sleep and eat far above timberline in the old days.

From the saddle there is a fairly distinct trail climbing east around the south end of the descending Wilson Peak ridge. Once around, climb northeast to the summit, staying just below the ridge on the east side until near the top. A short descent takes you over to the west side briefly in an exposed area, where some careful scrambling must be done. The top is just ahead.

From the top, the rest of the San Miguels are the near scene. Gladstone is southwest of Wilson Peak; the two are tied together by a narrow, rocky ridge. Gladstone, at 13,913 feet, just misses the fourteener class, but it is a tougher climb than Wilson Peak. The west side of Gladstone is marked by a deep gash that separates it from Mount Wilson; here lies one of the few glaciers in this part of the state. On the west side of the gash is a very high and rough ridge. Mount Wilson peaks out at the east end of it and El Diente at the west end. They are both great climbs but only for experienced climbers, or at least for parties with experienced leadership. The exposures at and near the top are awesome.

In the view to the southeast, the eye is immediately caught by Lizard Head, a shaft of rock rising 400 feet straight up out of the top of the mountain.

To the west is Dolores Peak and, still farther, Lone Cone. Beyond this radius to the north, east, and south are many high peaks too numerous to detail here. They display well the ruggedness of southwestern Colorado.

The return route from Wilson Peak is the same as the approach.

Another route for the climb deserves mention, but not full description. The starting and parking point is a little dirt road that turns west off Highway 145 about one and one-half miles south of the top of Lizard Head Pass. This route passes by the base of the Lizard Head shaft and into Bilk Basin for the ascent of Wilson Peak. This route is long and requires packing in overnight gear.

Handies Peak

Distance: *3 miles (round trip)*
Starting elevation: *11,600 feet*
Elevation gain: *2,448 feet*
High point: *14,048 feet*
Rating: *Moderate*
Time allowed: *3 to 4 hours*
Maps: *7.5'Handies Peak; 7.5'Redcloud Peak*

As fourteeners go, Handies is an easy one; it is rated a moderate hike only because of the altitude. But it is rewarding, because its summit provides an unrestricted view in all directions. The skylines here are tremendous, better than that of any city in the world, for there are hundreds of high peaks visible on a clear day, typical of the summer forenoons.

Handies is in a remote area. From Durango, you must go fifty miles on U.S. Highway 550 to Silverton, eight miles on rough gravel to Animas Forks, and seven miles on a very rough four-wheel-drive road to the start of the climb. Hikers with only two-wheel-drive vehicles will need to approach from the east via Colorado State Highway 149 through Lake City. I will describe the Silverton route first.

At the north end of Silverton's Greene Street (the main street of the town), turn right and follow Colorado State Road 110. This starts as pavement but soon turns to gravel. Follow this road about eight miles to a division, where the left side leads down along the river to the ghost town of Animas Forks, visible a half-mile ahead. You should take the right fork uphill and shift into four-wheel-drive. In less than a half-mile, the Cinnamon Pass Road turns off very sharply and steeply uphill to the right; it is so sharp that vehicles with longer wheelbases have to go past the turn, turn around in the road, and come back to it. This is a picturesque road above timberline, with high peaks and deep canyons to impress you with nature's ability in sculpturing. There

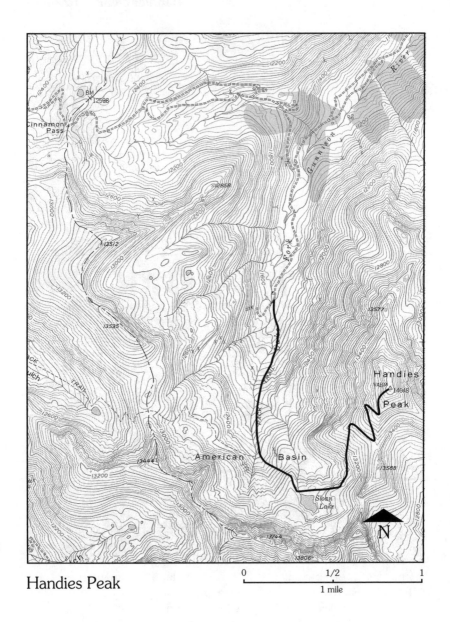

Handies Peak

0   1/2   1

1 mile

A fine columbine specimen with other wildflowers above timberline.

are also many wildflowers along the way, including the beautiful columbine, Colorado's state flower. Two and one-half miles up this road you top out at the pass at 12,600 feet. It is worth a stop here to look around and to thank your vehicle for having made it. Just over two miles down the other side, shortly after entering timber again, as you are rounding a left-turn switchback, a road turns off sharply to the right, downhill. There should be a sign indicating "American Basin." Take this road.

For the Lake City route, turn south along the west side of the valley about one and one-half miles southeast of the town of Lake City. This soon brings you along beautiful Lake San Cristobal. Beyond the lake, the road climbs several hundred feet above the Lake Fork of the Gunnison River and becomes the "shelf road," beautiful in its vistas, but steep and narrow in its traverse. Beyond the shelf, the road enters a more comfortable valley. As you are about to make the first switchback to start up Cinnamon Pass, you will come to the American Basin turnoff on the left. A quarter mile up this road brings you to a cut off of the road, where good parking is available. As you face south to the head of American Basin, you will see it walled off with high, broken cliffs—awesome bastions protecting the valley. The trail begins at the upper side of the parking lot and goes south over the old road for about a mile. It then turns uphill to the left off the old road. After a few hundred yards of steep trail, you drop into a small basin with a marshy bottom. The new trail swings to the right and climbs through talus up to Sloan Lake, a nice little gem in a rocky setting totally lacking in vegetation. The trail does not go directly to the lake, but a short side trail does; it is well worth taking. I understand it has some hungry trout in it.

The main trail swings back northeast over talus and in a quarter mile begins the final ascent, going north over tundra to the summit in about a mile of distance and a thousand feet of climb. Switchbacks at appropriate places make this one of the easiest final ascents of any of the fourteeners. The top is broad and relatively smooth.

There is a steep dropoff northeastward into Grizzly Gulch. Looking across this into and up the other side of the Lake Fork Valley to the massif, you will see Redcloud and Sunshine. Farther north on the horizon, you can see two more fourteeners— Wetterhorn (14,015 feet) and Uncompahgre (14,300 feet). To the west and a bit north, Sneffels (14,150 feet) should be the highest point on the skyline. To the south is a great host of other San Juan peaks.

The return trip is by the same route, although you could come straight west down the steep side of the mountain, taking care to avoid the few cliffs that are there.

An alternate route up Handies is directly out of the Lake Fork Valley up Grizzly Gulch. There is a good trail four miles to the top, starting at 10,400 feet and producing a total gain of 3,648 feet. This route is steeper and has more total altitude gain than the one described above. The trailhead is almost directly across the road from the Redcloud and Sunshine route. See below for that access.

Redcloud and Sunshine

Distance: *11.7 miles (round trip)*
Starting elevation: *10,400 feet*
Elevation gain: *4,634 feet (includes 1,000 feet lost and
         regained)*
High point: *14,034 feet*
Rating: *Difficult*
Time allowed: *7 to 8.5 hours*
Maps: *7.5' Redcloud Peak*

Redcloud and Sunshine are two fourteeners that are usually
climbed together. There is a 500-foot drop to the saddle
between, which is all that has to be regained to get the second
peak on the same trip. So here is a fairly easy way to bag two
fourteeners in one day. In fact, they are close enough to Handies
that strong parties, bent on making fast time, could do all three
in one day. The rating of difficult is given because of the distance
and total altitude gain, which are enough to tire even practiced
climbers. However, there is no really difficult spot anywhere
along this route.

To reach the trailhead, follow the same directions from
Silverton or Lake City given for Handies Peak, except go to
where Silver Creek crosses the Lake Fork Valley Road. The trailhead is four miles downstream from the American Basin turnoff;
it is where Grizzly and Silver Creek both come into Lake Fork.

On the northeast side of the road there is plenty of parking
space, in fact enough for good camping for those who want to
stay overnight and start out early in the morning. The cool water
of Silver Creek is just down the road a hundred yards. The trail
starts at this same spot and follows an old road for some distance, eventually emerging above the timber, where it follows
Silver Creek for about two miles along its left side. It eventually
crosses and spirals up the back side of Redcloud southward to a
saddle at 13,000 feet. At this point, the trail dips down the other
side. Abandon it; turn right and climb southwest up a ridge to its

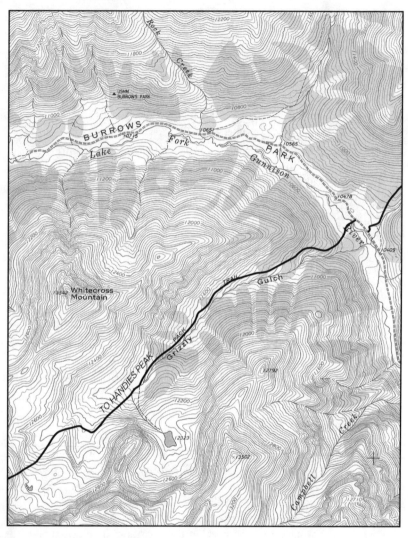

Redcloud and Sunshine

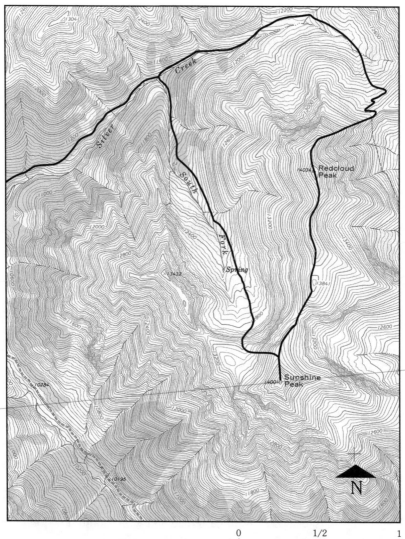

Many marmots can be seen above timberline and sometimes may even be approached, carefully.

top. Here, turn south and hike an easy two-tenths mile to the summit. Standing on the top, feast your eyes on peaks and valleys galore. The views are much the same as described for Handies, except that Sunshine looms large in the southern vista.

Marmots inhabit much of the backcountry high altitudes (9,000 feet or less and up). They are furry rodents with bushy tails and weigh about eight pounds. Because of their whistlelike call, they are nicknamed "whistle pigs." They like to sit up on their hind legs and stare at you or peek from behind a rock. Sometimes you can get within a few feet of them, but usually they quickly duck into a nearby hole that they have kept conveniently close to.

From Redcloud, it is an easy mile and a half south down into a saddle and out again up to the top of Sunshine.

For the return trip, it has become customary to shorten the distance by going back to the saddle north below Sunshine. About two miles can be saved this way. From the saddle, you can descend west 800 hundred feet quickly to the South Fork Valley and then go north about two miles over more gradually descending terrain, eventually rejoining the trail that you traversed on the uphill route (now a long distance below the top of Redcloud).

However, there are two serious problems with this route that have become more apparent in recent years. The steep descent has been causing serious erosion, and it is steep enough in an area of loose rocks that it is very easy for the uphill members of a party to loosen rocks and send them down dangerously toward the lower members of the party. This is bad enough that the Colorado Mountain Club has called upon its members and hike leaders doing this two-peak climb to stop using the saddle return. I agree with their concerns and endorse their restriction. This means going back over Redcloud and down the same trail you came up all the way, thus adding two miles to the total hike length and an extra 500 feet of climb, back up Redcloud. This is probably a good idea, and it will not add as much time to the hike as you might think. This is because the two miles through South Fork Valley are slower than they look because much of the route is over talus. Talus is not especially dangerous, but it is slow and sometimes tedious because you have to watch the placement of each step carefully. The first time I made this climb there were just two of us in the party, and we elected to start down the west side of Sunshine north of the summit but south of the saddle. We went diagonally down rather than straight down, as on the saddle route. This is still a fairly steep route, but the lead hiker is not directly below the follower. The two of us made it without any problem. A larger party might find it more of a problem.

This route does add one other difficulty. At the head of the valley is a length of low cliffs that is bypassed by the saddle route. There are a few ways to get through this by using scrambling techniques. The route back over Redcloud is definitely easier except for the added length. The distances and time given in the chart at the beginning of this description presuppose the return over Redcloud.

This is a one-day hike by any of these routes, but a long drive back to any launching point makes it advisable to consider car camping at the trailhead before an early morning start and perhaps even afterward, depending on the time taken.

Uncompahgre Peak, Matterhorn, Wetterhorn

Distance: *16 miles (round trip)*
Starting elevation: *11,000 feet*
Elevation gain: *3,309 feet*
High point: *14,309 feet*
Rating: *Moderate*
Time allowed: *7 to 8 hours*
Maps: *7.5' Uncompahgre; 7.5' Wetterhorn Peak;*
Uncompahgre National Forest

Uncompahgre Peak is a fourteener, one of the easiest in the state to climb, but the hike is quite long. As with all the fourteeners, it stands out above most of its surroundings, so the view from the top is certainly rewarding. Actually, it is the highest point in southwestern Colorado and the sixth highest peak in the state. The rating is moderate not because there are any difficulties, but only because of the altitude and length of the hike.

Uncompahgre has a very distinctive top that can easily be recognized from the east, the west, and the south. The top is very large and relatively smooth compared to most high peaks, being something close to 300 yards long and 100 yards wide and gently sloping to the southeast. This is the approach for the climb. The north face is, however, a complete contrast, plunging straight down nearly 1,000 feet. It is awesome!

The hike described here is the easy but long route.

Uncompahgre is in real backcountry. It is approached via a little road between Silverton and Lake City. From Lake City, take Henson Creek Road west out of town, and follow the creek to Capitol City nine miles west. This is a two-wheel-drive road.

The route from Silverton is over Engineer Pass, a four-wheel-drive road. Go northeast off the north end of Greene Street (the main street) out of Silverton. Follow this to the branch off to the right and uphill one-half mile south of Animas Forks. This is where the four-wheel-drive begins. Follow this north

Uncompahgre Peak.

4.8 miles to the top of Engineer Pass (12,800 feet). There is some beautiful country to be surveyed from the top of the pass, including the deep valley into which you are about to descend. It is nine miles down the east side of the pass to Capitol City.

Capitol City is a ghost town with a few old buildings still standing in the largest flat spot in Henson Creek Valley (several new houses have been built recently). Its mining founders of a hundred years ago were ambitious and dreamed of replacing Denver as the state capital.

At Capitol City, take a side road northwest two miles along the North Fork of Henson Creek to Matterhorn Creek. Turn right here, and drive as far as you can. A mile up this road is a vehicle barrier where all cars must stop; two-wheel-drives may have to stop a little short of this spot. If you want to car-camp, there are a few places along this way flat enough to use.

Hiking starts up the same road and soon gets above timberline. Stay to the right of the creek. As you reach higher ground in the openness of the tundra, you can begin to see the three high peaks of the area. Wetterhorn (14,015 feet) is to the left; Matterhorn (13,590 feet) is almost straight ahead; Uncompahgre, our objective, is off to the right.

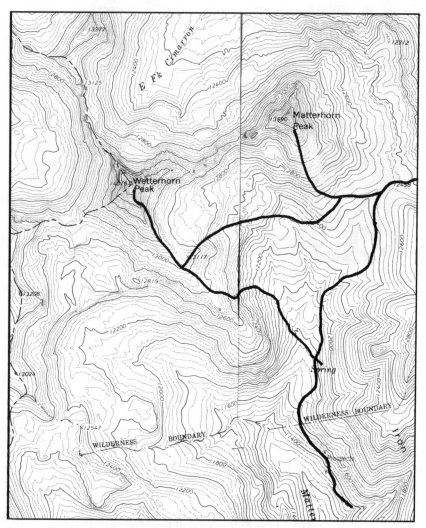

Uncompahgre Peak, Matterhorn, Wetterhorn

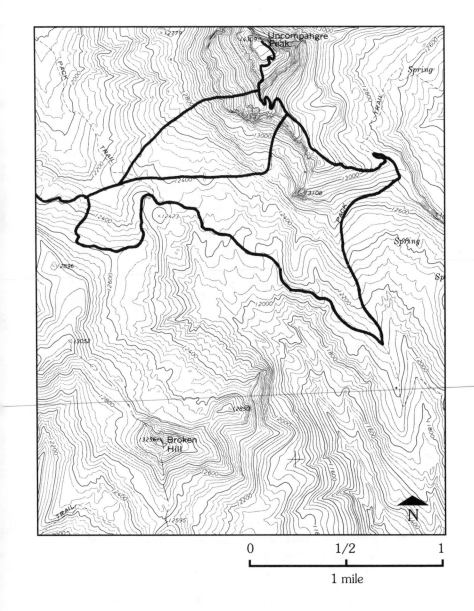

0   1/2   1

1 mile

Follow the trail to a saddle between Matterhorn and Uncompahgre, taking the right-hand side where the trails come in from the north. The Uncompahgre Trail swings back southeast for one and one-half miles beyond the saddle, joins a trail there going north another mile, and joins still another trail that ascends the southeast ridge, at first westerly and then northwesterly another mile to the top. This is a long, gradual, easy route.

An alternative route can cut off as much as two miles but is much steeper. It is worth it to many hikers for the time saved. At the Matterhorn-Uncompahgre saddle where the trail starts southeast, abandon it and strike out northeast toward the mountain itself. There are two ways it can be climbed from the west side, neither of which is a trail. There is a large notch one-half mile south of the summit filled with steep talus (visible in photograph on page 235). The route works well, though some of the rocks near the top are loose enough to require some care. Once over the top of this, on the solid again, you will find the trail ascending from the southeast. Join it for an easy half-mile to the top—not too easy, though, for it includes another 900 feet of altitude gain.

The other west side way is north of this notch and the large cliffs near it. Choose a route far enough to the left of these cliffs to aim for a point just south of the top, where there is a break in the last two bands of summit cliffs. This route is quite steep, but it will work all right. You will be on tundra part of the time and loose rock part of the time. It is the fastest route from the west side. The last time I climbed in this area, a friend and I used this route; it was short enough that we were able to climb Uncompahgre, Matterhorn, and Wetterhorn all in one day. This would not have been possible using either of the other routes.

Once on top, you are "king of the mountain," for this is the highest point in the area, and you can see many miles in all directions on a good day, and vast stretches of peaks and big valleys. The nearest peaks, of course, are Matterhorn, which you can now look down on, and Wetterhorn. To the north of Wetterhorn is Coxcomb, so named because of the appearance of its unique top.

The descent is best made by the approach route. One of the others given here would work, but the two west-side routes are hard to pick out from above if you did not come up one of them.

Strong parties who are intent on "peak bagging" can climb one or both of the other two peaks in the group in the same day, assuming they are qualified. Matterhorn is no problem. It can be climbed by bushwhacking up the southeast side on the way back from Uncompahgre. It is steep tundra at first; this gives way to large rocks—some loose, some fixed—as you get within 500 or 600 feet from the top. In some locations, Matterhorn would be an impressive peak, but here it is subdued by its two higher neighbors. The most impressive view here is the ridge on the west side connecting to Wetterhorn. This is a jagged knife-edge a mile long. Just looking at it can be scary.

Wetterhorn is not recommended for novices without experienced leadership, for the last sixty feet or more are very steep. There are good small toeholds and handholds, but unfortunately, many of these are covered with sand and gravel, giving a very treacherous surface. A fixed rope in this area is a good idea for safety.

For those who want to climb Wetterhorn after doing Matterhorn and/or Uncompahgre, the following route is recommended. Drop down below Matterhorn to the southwest to about 12,600 feet and go west to the ridge running southeast from Wetterhorn. You could stay higher near the connecting ridge, but this is not profitable because it is so full of big boulders that it makes tedious, slow going. Mount straight up the southeast ridge; at the top, strike northwest toward the summit. There is a well-worn path most of this way. At about 100 feet below the summit is a very nice pocket big enough to accommodate a good-sized party. There is a high wall on the west side and good shelter from wind all the way around. It makes a fine rest-and-snack stopping place. The top of Wetterhorn is much smaller than that of Uncompahgre. The north side, like Uncompahgre, is a sheer drop.

For the descent, go back down the southeast ridge about a mile and drop off the east side. (The south end has cliffs that cannot be interpreted very well from above.) Across the stream at the bottom, you should soon pick up the trail that you came up earlier in the day for the return to your parking place.

The mileage and rating given in the heading are for Uncompahgre only. If Matterhorn and Wetterhorn are done also, add 2.8 more miles and 2,500 feet more of ascent. The rating in this case would be hard.

The Colorado Trail

Since publication of the first edition of this book, the Colorado Trail has become a reality and is definitely a part of hiking in southwest Colorado. It was conceived and actually started in the mid-1970s but soon languished, and the original organization developing it fell apart. The idea nearly died until three groups got together and combined sponsorship: The U.S. Forest Service, one of the originators of the concept and an enthusiastic booster from the first; the Friends of the Colorado Trail, a group organized specifically for planning and promoting construction of the trail; and the Colorado Mountain Club.

Gudy Gaskill was appointed chairperson of the Club's Trail and Huts Committee. She began work on the trail, using all-volunteer labor. The plan was to use existing trails as much as possible and to work out new connections between them. For special reasons existing trails might be bypassed, and were, in a few cases. Progress was still slow, but moving; some people were pessimistic, expressing doubt that the trail would ever be completed. Eventually the project came to the attention of Richard Lamm, then governor of Colorado and an avid hiker and jogger. He and Gudy Gaskill got together and planned to complete the trail within two years with all-volunteer labor. Gudy put a prodigious amount of effort into organizing work teams and putting them on their assignments. In the last full summer nearly a thousand volunteers were at work. The U.S. Forest Service gave excellent support.

The trail was completed in time for ceremonies marking the event in Durango and Denver in September 1987. It was completed only in the sense that all trails used were connected at that time. But work has continued since then, on a smaller scale, in improving some sections that were hardly recognizable as trail in 1987, and in making spur trails to provide many good access points throughout the state.

The Colorado Trail is 474 miles long, beginning just outside Durango and ending just outside Denver. Southwest Colorado is fortunate in having a high percentage of these miles, because the trail must do a lot of winding to get through the rugged San Juan Mountains. There are seventy-eight miles of the trail in the Animas District (where Durango is located) of the San Juan National Forest alone.

Natives surveying the neighborhood's visitors.

The Colorado Trail is a backpacker's paradise, but this book is dedicated to the day-hiker; fortunately, several sections of the trail in southwest Colorado are quite usable for this purpose. Some places can even function as partial loop routes where you can leave a car at each end. I will therefore describe access points and suggested day hikes in this area. The hiker who wants to backpack longer sections of the trail should get the official guidebook written by Randy Jacobs, entitled simply *The Colorado Trail,* and published by The Colorado Trail Foundation. There is also a complete set of topo maps, with the trail imposed, to go with the guidebook, although the maps are sold separately. Both are invaluable to the serious hiker of the trail. One small disadvantage for the Durango hiker is that Denver is taken as the starting point, so from there the book and maps have to be read backward. It is helpful that mileages are given by sections. The latest issue of the San Juan National Forest map also has the trail on it as a tiny dashed red line—hard to see but usable.

The heading information given with the following access points is only meant as a general guide, because individual hikers and groups will want to choose their own distances rather than feel obligated to go to the next access point for which distances and elevations are given. This also affects the ratings because distances are a factor in how hard a hike may be.

First Access—The Trailhead

Distance: *To Gudy's Rest, 4 miles*
To Second Access (Sliderock Trail), *18 miles*
Starting elevation: *6,900 feet*
Elevation gain: *To Gudy's Rest, 1,040 feet*
To Second Access: *3,380 feet*
High point: *At Gudy's Rest, 8,000 feet*
At Second Access: *10,340 feet*
Rating: *To Gudy's Rest, easy to moderate*
To Second Access: *Hard (only because of long distance)*
Time allowed: *To Gudy's Rest, 5 hours (round trip)*
To Second Access: *7 to 10 hours (one way)*
Maps: *7.5' Durango West; 7.5' Monument Hill; San Juan National Forest; Jacobs Maps 29, 28 (the Jacobs maps are from the first edition and may vary a bit from the later editions)*

The trail begins a few miles west of Durango. To get there, go to Twenty-Fifth Street and turn west off Main; at the edge of town it becomes Junction Creek Road. Follow it from Main three and one-half miles to the national forest; just across the cattle-guard that marks the boundary the trail begins downhill in 100 feet. There is parking here for a few cars. The trail follows close along the creek for more than a mile.

Another entry option is to take the road west and uphill for a mile and a quarter, where there is a sharp switchback to the northeast; just beyond this is a good Forest Service campground. At the switchback there is more parking space than at the trail-head. You can begin hiking west here, and in the meadow below you will soon strike the trail. From here it goes on nearly a mile before crossing the stream over a good forest service bridge, and then begins a series of switchbacks up the steep canyonside. At the top there is a nice rest area with a bench, called "Gudy's Rest," for viewing down the valley toward Durango. This is about four miles from the trail beginning.

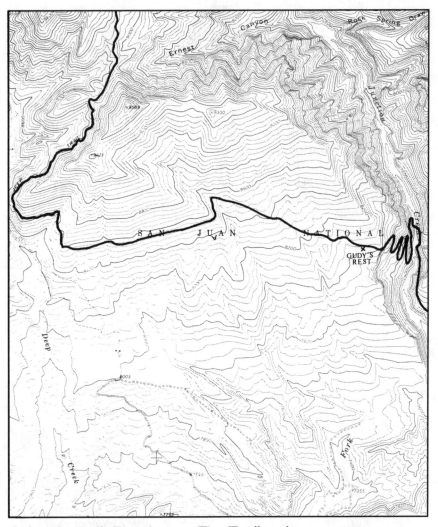

Colorado Trail, First Access–The Trailhead

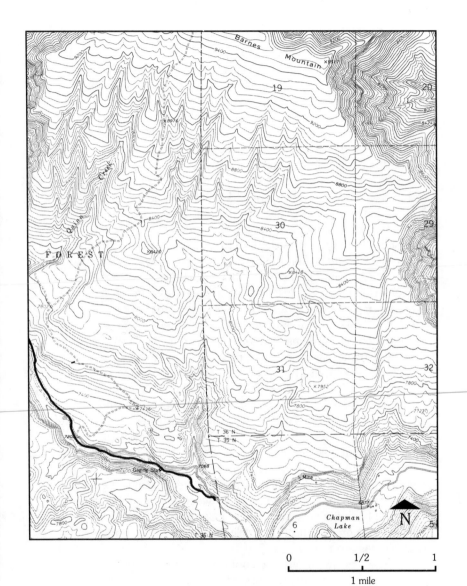

The trail above here climbs gradually for several miles before again descending gradually into Junction Creek canyon. This begins rugged country. From here on there is quite a bit of up and down, mostly up, arriving in eighteen miles from the trailhead at the next possible road access. This is the beginning of the Sliderock Trail, covered earlier in the description for Kennebec Pass–Taylor Lake (see page 78). This is more than most people want to do in a day hike, especially since the trail starts at 6,960 feet; the Sliderock trailhead is at 10,340 feet for a net gain of 3,380 feet, and more than that counting the downhill distances that have to be regained. This is beautiful big-timber and mountain country.

For the return, most people elect to go back from Gudy's Rest by the way they came, but there are a couple more options. The new Hoffeins Connection Trail comes up to the Colorado Trail just beyond Gudy's Rest. You can take it down to the Dry Creek Road in 1.9 miles. The other option is to go up the Colorado Trail another 2.6 miles to where the Dry Fork Trail comes up. It will take you back down to the Dry Creek Road at the same place as Hoffeins Connection in 3.9 miles. These are point-to-point hikes, necessitating a car at both ends. For a full explanation of these trails, see the Dry Fork Loop, page 42.

NOTE: The Colorado Trail maps are continuous in order to show all of the Colorado Trail within southwest Colorado as it is treated in this book. This should make the trail easier to interpret and serves also as a help to longer-distance backpackers. Because of the continuousness of these maps, one of them—the map that covers the distance between Taylor Lake and Hotel Draw—is not very useful for the day hiker (unless that person puts in a very long day) because of the distance between access points. Hikers coming from the west side up the Roaring Fork Road will find this map more practical than will hikers coming from the southern or eastern roads.

The placement of these continuous maps presents a dilemma. They could all be placed together at the end of the chapter, but it seems more useful to keep each section close to its relevant account. Thus, I have elected to show maps after each access description. This will sometimes make it necessary for the reader of a particular access account to refer to the map for the access immediately preceding or following it in order to study the entire route of interest.

Second Access—Sliderock Trail

Distance: *To Third Access, 3 miles (round trip)*
Starting elevation: *10,240 feet*
Elevation gain: *1,520 feet*
High point: *Kennebec Pass, 11,760 feet*
Rating: *Moderate*
Time allowed: *2 to 3 hours*
Maps: *7.5' Monument Hill; 7.5' La Plata; San Juan National Forest; Jacobs 28, 29*

The Colorado Trail crosses the road at the beginning of the Sliderock Trail. This trail is uphill from here and is described as Kennebec Pass–Taylor Lake (see page 78). That route and its access will not be repeated here. Downhill plunges immediately into big timber and descends rapidly. This is described in the preceding account beginning at the trailhead. You might want to try this entire eighteen miles downhill, leaving a car at beginning and end. There is some uphill travel on this route, but it is mainly down. Even so, with no lengthy stops it will still be a long day. After a couple of miles there are several fords of the stream to be made, and during the heavy snowmelt season this could be quite difficult. Shorter distances will be easier.

The map shows a possible loop course. For this route, hike down the Colorado Trail to Gaines (or Leavenworth) Gulch. There should be an old road there that leads up to Neglected Mine and on out to the main road. I do not know whether the trail and the road actually intersect, but the map looks as if they do. It is about three miles on to the road, with the mine at the midpoint. At the main road it is still some five miles back to your starting point; you may want to leave a car at each spot.

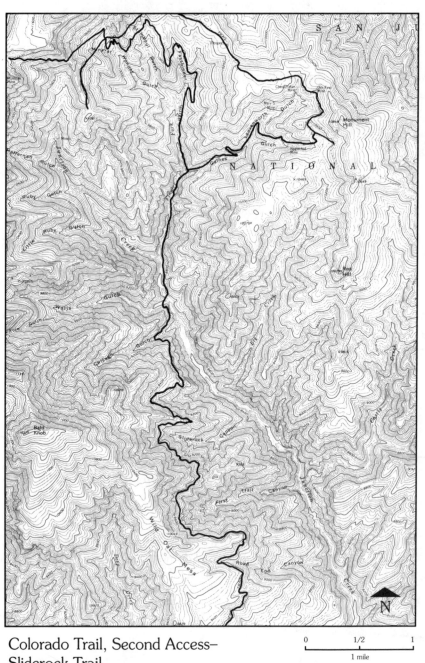

Colorado Trail, Second Access–
Sliderock Trail

Third Access—La Plata Canyon

Distance*: *To Taylor Lake, 2.5 miles (round trip)*
To Fifth Access (Hotel Draw Road): *20 miles (one way)*
Starting elevation: *11,620 feet*
Elevation loss to Taylor Lake: *60 feet*
Elevation gain to high point (north of Taylor Lake): *718 feet*
High point en route to Hotel Draw (second ridgepoint north of Taylor Lake): *12,338 feet*
Rating: *To Taylor Lake, Easy; to Hotel Draw, Hard, only because of distance*
Time allowed*: *To Taylor Lake (round trip), 1.5 hours; to Hotel Draw (one way), 10 to 14 hours*
Maps: *7.5' La Plata; 7.5' Monument Hill; San Juan National Forest; Jacobs Map 28*
*Several optional routes are given in the text that will increase variations in distances and times in the foregoing chart.

This is basically the trail described as Kennebec Pass–Taylor Lake (see page 78), except with a different access point: the La Plata Canyon road. This road starts north off U.S. Highway 160 ten and one-half miles west of Durango and a quarter-mile west of the Hesperus Post Office. Follow this road twelve and one-half miles, at which point it turns sharply right across the La Plata River near its headwaters. The river is a small stream here. People with two-wheel-drives should park here and begin hiking. It is quite rough above this point, but four-wheel-drives can make it another steep mile and a half to the end of the road, where there is a level saddle with plenty of parking and a great panoramic view of San Juan peaks. The Colorado Trail crosses the saddle at this point. It arrives from the east over the Sliderock Trail from Kennebec Pass and goes on west of here toward Taylor Lake and then over the Highline Trail.

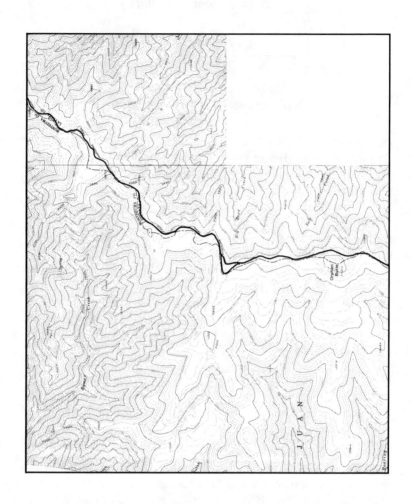

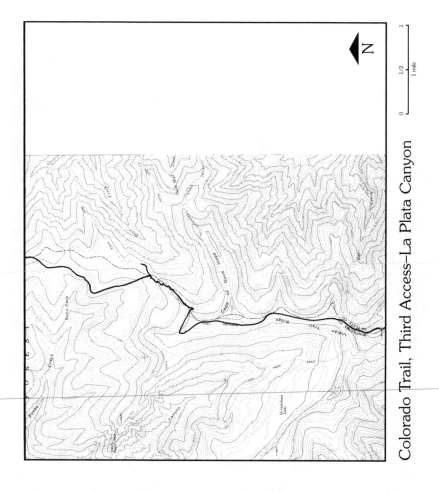

Colorado Trail, Third Access–La Plata Canyon

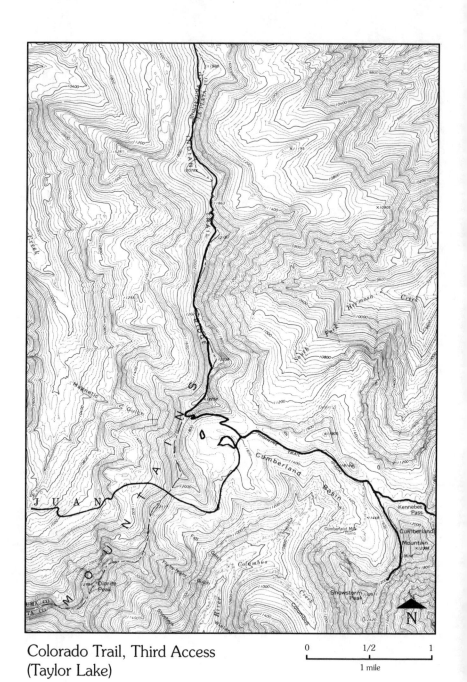

Colorado Trail, Third Access
(Taylor Lake)

0   1/2   1

1 mile

The road over to the Notch from the Colorado Trail at the top of La Plata Canyon.

You can begin hiking here. To the right (southeast) in 300 yards the trail splits; straight ahead in a mile is the "Notch." This can be taken in a four-wheel-drive or hiked. At the Notch there is only room to park two cars—very carefully—but it is a side trip well worth doing. The wildflowers on the steep mountainside above the road are glorious, with many varieties vying for attention. The terrain drops off below the road at just less than cliff pitch into Cumberland Basin. Down the other side of the Notch the view is dramatic. You can look down into the diverse drainages that come together to make Junction Creek and on over a vast forested area into the Animas Valley and the city of Durango in the distance far below; Fort Lewis College is located on a shelf just beyond and above the city. The Colorado Trail has come up to your level through all this difficult territory. It is one of the toughest long stretches of the entire trail. Nearer at hand, the road goes down on the right in a half-mile to the Bessie G Mine. When that mine is working, as it is from time to time, the Notch road is closed to public vehicular traffic from its beginning at the saddle. At this writing, the road is open.

When you start from the saddle toward the Notch, you come in 300 yards to an old road, now closed to vehicles, swinging off to the left. This is the route of the Colorado Trail; it goes shortly through Kennebec Pass and down the Sliderock Trail to its origin, given above as the second access point and described from the other end.

If you start hiking west from the saddle parking spot you come in a little over a mile to Taylor Lake, a lovely spot in a mountain cirque. The lake is stocked for fishing. Just before reaching the lake, the trail splits. The right fork is the Highline Trail, which is followed here by the Colorado Trail. It soon begins to climb steeply, reaching the ridge 500 feet above the lake in a half-mile. Here the trail swings north and follows the ridge for many miles, passing over or just below several ridge points before reaching the Roaring Fork Road that comes up from the Dolores River Valley on the west. This point is already well beyond day-hike range, so you will want to turn around somewhere earlier on the ridge. The first several miles of the ridge are above 12,000 feet.

Another optional route is at the split just before the lake. The left fork here becomes the Sharkstooth Trail and soon brings you to the lake, but it goes on south for a half-mile and then west another half-mile, where it crosses the ridge below 12,000 feet and enters the head of Bear Creek Canyon. On around farther the trail splits again; the right-hand side drops into the canyon and follows Bear Creek many miles through rugged territory to the Dolores River— definitely backpacking distance. At the split where Bear Creek Trail goes down and right, Sharkstooth Trail continues straight, crossing the head of the canyon below Diorite Peak and going on over to the pass between Sharkstooth Peak and Centennial Peak. At this point you are approximately five miles from your car; you may want to turn back, but you could go on down the other side for a mile and a half to the Sharkstooth trailhead, where you might want to have another car waiting. See the Centennial Peak and Sharkstooth description (page 89) for this access.

All of this area is great country with great views in many places. It also offers many climbing opportunities. In addition to

Centennial and Sharkstooth as climbing options, closer to your parking place are Cumberland Mountain on the north side of the Notch and Snowstorm on its south side. The latter peak can be climbed from some point just through the Notch wherever it is not too steep to get started; there is also an old trail that starts eastward above the Bessie G Mine, then it swings south through a pass with Lewis Mountain. This offers an easier route than starting at the Notch. At the pass, turn right and climb back up the ridge to the Snowstorm summit. Cumberland is best climbed from its west ridge, starting at the Kennebec turnoff from the Notch road. You could also climb it going south from Kennebec Pass. On the north side of the pass is a short climb to the top of an unnamed ridge that offers excellent views from the high point near its north end. Also, just on the east side of the pass, you can hike a quarter-mile southeast along an old road to the Muldoon Mine, now abandoned. The views down the valley are similar to those at the Notch. One interesting artifact left here is an outhouse that hangs out over the edge of the abyss below; unfortunately for the user, it faces away from the view.

Still one more hike from your parking place is a short one worth exploring. At the west side of the parking area this route follows an old road just to the right of the Taylor Lake route. It goes two-thirds of a mile around a low ridge to an old quarry. This opens up more northwesterly vistas, including Lizard Head and the San Miguels (including Mount Wilson, Wilson Peak, and El Diente, all fourteeners).

NOTE: The heading chart with this access gives data all the way to the Hotel Draw Road for anyone brave enough to try its twenty miles in one day. It can be hiked south to north just as easily, perhaps even more easily due to a higher starting altitude. Also, to make this section of the Colorado Trail easier, one can split it into two day hikes of fourteen and six miles. The split can be made some six miles south of the Hotel Draw access to where Forest Service Road 564 leaves the ridge and starts down toward Dolores. See a more detailed description of the trail section from Hotel Draw to the top of La Plata Canyon under Fifth Access (see page 256).

Fourth Access—Sharkstooth Trail

I only need to call attention to this as an access point for the Colorado Trail that is suitable for those who want to come in from the west. It has already been described sufficiently as Centennial Peak and Sharkstooth (see page 89), and above as Third Access. It has the disadvantage of requiring about five miles of hiking (although through very worthwhile territory) before reaching the Colorado Trail at Taylor Lake. At that point it can be hiked north or east.

Fifth Access—Bolam Pass and
Hotel Draw (Eastern)—Scotch Creek,
Roaring Fork, and Barlow Creek (Western)—
South Mineral Creek (Northern)

Starting elevation*: *11,800 feet (Bolam Pass)*
Rating: *Easy to hard (depending on route choice and distance)*
Maps: *7.5' Hermosa Peak; San Juan National Forest; Jacobs Maps 26, 25, 27*
*Too many options are given in the following text to account for any more summarizing in the usual chart form. See the text for distances and key altitudes.

Bolam Pass and Hotel Draw are two separate locations on the Colorado Trail, but they are approached by the same road. To get there, go to the Purgatory Ski Area twenty-eight miles north of Durango; turn in and go to the northeast corner of the parking lot. Take the graveled road (Forest Service 578) north from the lot. Under dry conditions, two-wheel-drive cars can usually make this road, but it is a bit rough at the upper end; the last pitch before the ghost town of Graysill is quite steep. Weaker cars without a good low gear could have trouble here. Having to park below this grade, however, would not be disastrous, for it would add less than a mile of hiking up to the Colorado Trail.

Above Purgatory the road climbs rapidly through many switchbacks until it reaches the top of the ridge above the ski area, where it makes a right-angle turn to the north and begins to descend a little. In four-tenths of a mile from this turn there is a left-hand turn downhill from the road; take this down into a lovely valley called Hermosa Park. The northern runs of the ski area will be visible across the valley to the south (left) a little way down. In a few miles you are across this valley and can start north along the Hermosa Creek. In a mile or so you have to ford the creek. It is wide here, and the spring snowmelt makes it inadvisable to cross. Usually by the third week of June it is okay, but two-wheel-drive cars may have to wait a bit longer, until it is less than six to eight inches deep. It has a rocky bottom and can be made then by two-wheel-drives if driven resolutely and not too slowly. High clearance helps, too. In about a mile above the ford, the Hotel Draw road turns off left. For the Bolam Pass route go straight ahead here. I will describe this route first and then come back to Hotel Draw.

The pass road continues for several miles, staying near or above the creek and eventually climbing through several switchbacks to the ghost town of Graysill, which is located at the edge of a ledge. It is worth stopping here to look around the settlement, where most of the buildings are now collapsed or gone; this is also a good place to look back over the valley through which you have just come and on south to the La Plata Mountains. By this time you are at almost 11,000 feet, after a climb of more than 2,000, so a lot of scenic beauty opens up below. The road goes on and quickly makes a swing around to the left, climbing to another flat spot where there is a little lake on the left. This is a mile below the top of Bolam Pass, and here the Colorado Trail crosses the road; in fact, by the time you get to the lake you have already crossed it. Go back a bit and park in the clear area to the east side of the lake. You can take the trail in either direction from here. Across the road there should be a cairn to mark the trail. Pick it up here and start moving northeast. The trail soon joins another road; in about a third of a mile it swings right at a right angle over another old road, now closed

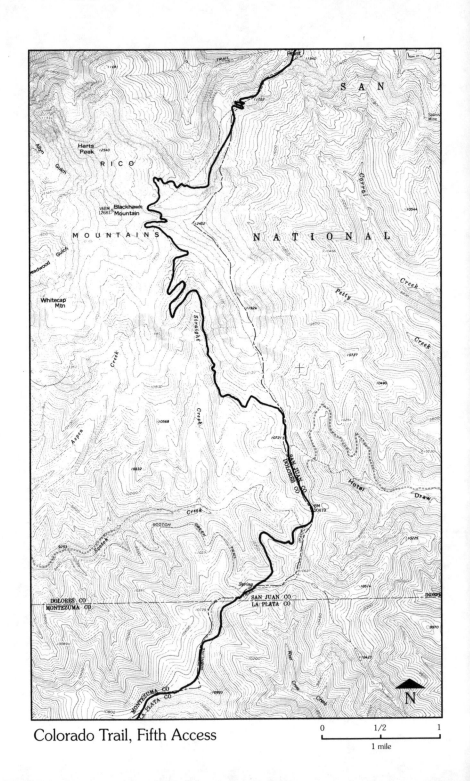

Colorado Trail, Fifth Access

0   1/2   1

1 mile

to vehicles. In a short distance it moves out of the forest and gradually uphill along a route marked by posts to a crossing of Sliderock Ridge, which is descending from Grizzly Peak; here it follows the Highline Trail. On the other side of the ridge the trail swings north and northeast. In another five miles it descends to a crossing of Cascade Creek below Grizzly Peak and then climbs out to an unnamed pass south of South Mineral Creek Campground (see "South Mineral Creek–Cascade" on page 179). It crosses the Rico-Silverton Trail at the top of this pass and goes on around to Little Molas Lake in another eleven-plus miles, definitely a backpack distance. The pass is nine miles from the parking spot. Day-hikers will want to turn around before this, probably at or before crossing Cascade Creek. There are no great objectives along this portion of the trail, but much of it is above timberline and affords many fine vistas.

The Rico-Silverton Trail also is a suitable access route if taken from the north, going toward this pass. Pick it up at the South Mineral Creek Campground and hike south or, better yet, drive the four-wheel-drive road south to the Bandora Mine and hike south from there (for this route see "South Mineral Creek–Cascade" on page 179). You will strike the Colorado Trail at the pass, three miles of gradual climb from the mine. West on the trail from here is toward Grizzly Peak and Bolam Pass; east is toward the Twin Sisters and on around toward Little Molas Lake.

Back at the parking place you can take the southwesterly direction of the Colorado Trail along the side of the little lake. In a hundred yards it enters the trees, where it may be more distinct than in the grassy area along the lake. In the first mile it climbs a couple hundred feet and comes out into the flat meadow north of Hermosa Peak, then it joins a road coming southwest from the Bolam Pass road. It follows this road for more than a mile, passing along the rocky side of Hermosa Peak. Where the road curves around to head straight south, the trail takes off to the right (west) climbing into the woods. In about three miles, after some up and down travel, it rises to a pass at 12,000 feet between Blackhawk Mountain, less than a half-mile west, and an unnamed sharp point a third of a mile east. Blackhawk, at 12,681 feet, is an easy climb up the ridge from the pass. The unnamed point is quite steep from here and more easily climbed from its south descending ridge.

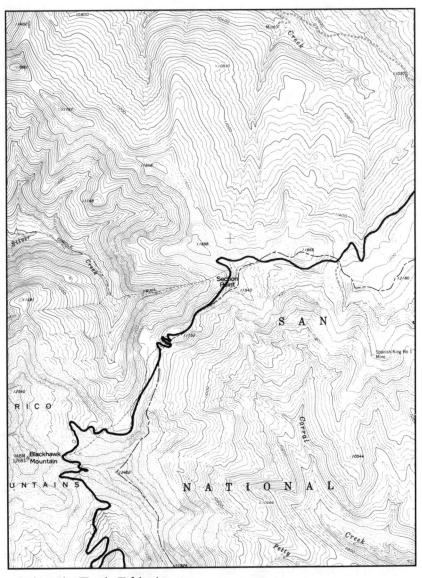

Colorado Trail, Fifth Access

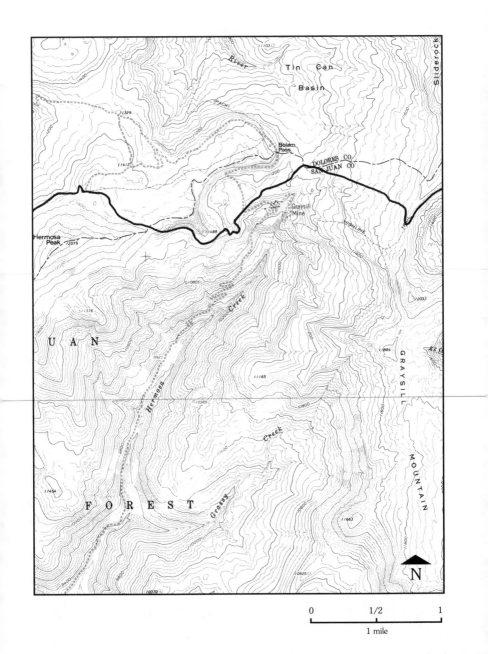

River   Tin   Can

Basin

11103

Sliderock

11329

(PACK)

11412

11200

Bolam
Pass

DOLORES CO
SAN JUAN CO

Graysill
Mine

HIGHLINE

Hermosa
Peak   12575

11488

11400

12033

U A N

511376

9921

11884

GRAYSILL

010805

Hermosa

Creek

11165

010385

Grassy   Creek

10900

11454

F O R E S T

11663

MOUNTAIN

10925

10370

N

0   1/2   1

1 mile

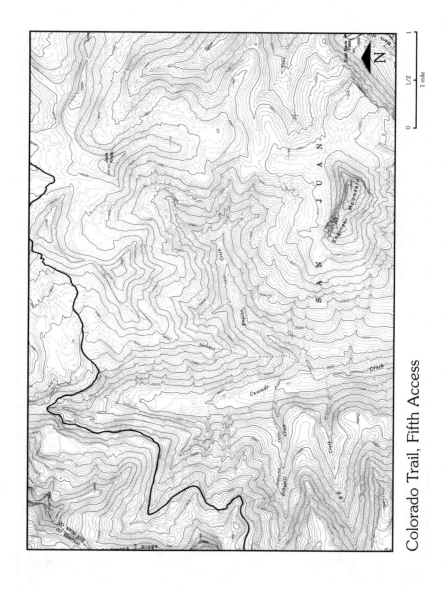

Colorado Trail, Fifth Access

The Colorado Trail as it crosses the saddle below, with Blackhawk Mountain beyond.

There are other climbing opportunities you may want to consider in addition to Blackhawk. Behind it, from northwest to southwest, are Harts Peak (12,540 feet), Dolores Mountain (12,112 feet), and Whitecap Mountain (12,376 feet). Around to the south and then east there are a couple of unnamed points at 11,362 feet and 11,685 feet. All or most of these could be done in one day, especially if you drive on over Bolam Pass and down the road to the barrier a short distance northwest of Hermosa Peak. A friend and I did this in 1989 and encountered some extra hazards before the day was over—rain, mud, and, for a half-hour, blinding snow.

The pass east of Blackhawk is just short of seven miles from the parking spot. If you want to go on you will reach the Hotel Draw road in just over five miles. The trail descends rapidly, later regaining some altitude before getting to the road. You might want to have a car parked here instead of hiking back.

Before turning to the Hotel Draw description, I want to mention that the Bolam Pass access can also be reached from the west out of the Dolores River Valley via the Barlow Creek Road (Forest Service 578). It turns east off State Highway 145

about halfway between Lizard Head Pass and the town of Rico,
roughly five miles from both. At the turnoff the road immediately
crosses the river and then passes, on the left, the access to a nice
forest service campground on the river, a good overnight spot if
you need it. The road then climbs about seven miles (the last two
are quite rough, making four-wheel-drive advisable) to a flat opening in the forest; soon after this the road splits. The right side
swings east and then south to a barrier near Hermosa Peak. The
Colorado Trail joins this road just beyond the barrier. The left
side turns sharply over an arroyo and goes north over the top of
Bolam Pass. It reaches the little lake where the trail is located
about two miles from the turnoff. From this direction it is the second little lake; it is quite close to the first.

As noted, the Hotel Draw road (Forest Service 550) turns
left off the Bolam Pass road about a mile beyond the ford of Hermosa Creek. It soon moves into the next valley and then starts a
steep ascent, reaching the top of the ridge through switchbacks
in about three miles. Here it meets the Colorado Trail at 10,419
feet. A little parking area can be found
nearby. This is the same spot mentioned above, and the
route north is the same, five miles to the Blackhawk Pass.
The peak climbs mentioned can also be done from this starting
point. In addition, the ridge that culminates in the sharp point
on the east side of Blackhawk Pass rises, beginning only
one mile in from the road, on this northerly approach on the
trail. It is an easy climb to that point this way, but over two miles
longer. At the base of this ridge the trail splits. The Colorado
Trail turns left, avoiding the ridge; the Highline Trail goes on up
the ridge a way before dropping off the left side and rejoining the
Colorado Trail about two miles farther up—a little way below the
pass. For the point climb, stay on the ridge even where the trail
starts down.

At the trail crossing where you park, the road goes south.
The Scotch Creek road (still FS 550) soon turns right and descends in several miles to the Dolores River Valley and Colorado
State Highway 145, about two miles south of Rico. Access from
the west to the Colorado Trail is possible from this route. This is
a four-wheel-drive road, quite good at the top but rough farther
down; there are a lot of aspen at the upper levels. Hotel Draw
across Scotch Creek makes a very nice autumn-color drive in

early October; on down the Dolores Valley to the town of Dolores is beautiful, too.

Where Scotch Creek turns west, the other road (now FS 564) goes south. In about six miles, after some winding around, the road begins to veer more to the west and descends into the Dolores Valley over what is now the Roaring Fork Road (435), joining Highway 145 about six miles farther below (southwest) Scotch Creek. Roaring Fork (435 and 564) is a good gravel road and makes a good access from the west that is usable by most cars. The map shows six survey miles to the trail, but the winding it does makes the road close to twice this long. From the top of Hotel Draw the Colorado Trail goes south along the ridge, most of the time at or near the road, for nearly the same six miles. Where the road turns west, the trail goes straight on south toward Orphan Butte (a tree-covered point 200 feet high), just over a mile distant. For the entire distance from the top of Hotel Draw the trail follows at or near the top of the ridge with a gradual net altitude rise of 1,919 feet. It continues on south along the ridge, now called Indian Trail Ridge, in eleven-plus miles to Taylor Lake, and in another mile east to the top of La Plata Canyon, which is discussed as Third Access on page 249. The highest spot on this route is next to the last ridgepoint at 12,338 feet; it comes shortly before the descent to Taylor Lake, three-quarters of a mile away by the trail. Round-trip, this would be too long for a day hike, but a car left at the saddle above La Plata Canyon would make it a more practical, though still lengthy, day trip.

Sixth Access—Molas Pass

Distance: *West to Twin Sisters, 16 miles (round trip); east to the Animas River: 10 miles (round trip)*
Starting elevation at Molas Pass: *10,919 feet*
Elevation gain: *West to Twin Sisters, 881 feet; east (return trip from the Animas River), 1,989 feet*
High point west: *11,800 feet at base of Twin Sisters*
High point east: *10,919 feet at Molas Pass*
Low point east: *8,930 feet at Animas River*
Rating: *West, easy in climbing but hard because of distance to Twin Sisters and back; East, moderate but tiring because of return climb out of Animas Canyon*
Time allowed: *West, 8 to 10 hours for full round trip; East, 5 to 7 hours*
Maps: *7.5' Snowdon Peak; San Juan National Forest; Jacobs Maps 25, 24*

The Colorado Trail crosses U.S. Highway 550 a couple hundred yards north of the top of this pass, which is located seven and one-half miles south of Silverton, about forty-two miles north of Durango. There is a good rest stop at the top of the pass for a nice overlook to the north and east. A paved parking area and restrooms are also available. However, the parking should be used only for temporary overlook users. All-day hikers should look elsewhere for parking.

The western route is described first. After climbing a little grade you go downhill and around the south end of Little Molas Lake and then start north around to the west side of the lake. Here the trail crosses a gravel road and starts a steady climb to the west. Since this is about a mile of relatively uninteresting hiking from the highway, I suggest you consider driving to this point, where there is good parking away from the busy pass. To do so, drive down the Silverton side of the pass four-tenths of a mile to a left turn on a gravel road. This winds around about a mile before coming to the trail on the west side of Little Molas and about fifty feet above the lake. There is adequate parking here, also good camping and fishing administered by the Forest Service. The trail starts west, zigzags upward, swings south and then back north, climbing gradually all the while. At about three miles from the lake it swings west across a mild saddle, at 11,600 feet, that separates Bear Creek drainage to the north and North Lime Creek to the south. Shortly before the saddle it passes under a high unnamed point that is part of the massif that becomes Grand Turk and Sultan Mountain farther north. After the crossing it stays pretty close to this same level while passing under some more high unnamed points, eventually passing under Twin Sisters and, later, Grizzly Peak on its way to Bolam Pass, about twenty miles from Little Molas, a good two- or three-day backpack. Twin Sisters are eight miles from the lake, a good place to turn around on a day hike if you do not do so before. Much of this trail is above timberline, affording good views to the south, southeast, and southwest.

The eastern route basically follows the Molas Trail already described (see page 131); however, the starting point is not the same. If you start at the pass on the highway you add a mile and a quarter and about 350 feet of altitude to the hike. It descends in a series of switchbacks to a union with the Molas Trail a quarter-mile below that trail's beginning, then it follows the same route all the way down to the Animas River, more than 1,500 feet below; the final plunge is taken in more than two dozen switchbacks. It then crosses the river over a good footbridge, goes down the railroad track (south) a couple hundred yards, then climbs out the east side over the Elk Creek Trail, reaching the Continental Divide in eight and three-quarter miles. The finish is up a great mountainside over a series of many switchbacks. At the top you will join the Eldorado Lake route. This is much too far for a day hike, but if you want to backpack it you could go north along that trail (see "Continental Divide," page 204). In this case you need to have your second car at the head of Cunningham Gulch. This would make a fine two- to three-day backpack through great country and a variety of terrain with stately trees, spectacular peaks, the river, lakes, and tundra above timberline. Most day-hikers will want to turn around at the river, because the return trip involves a steep and tiring climb out.

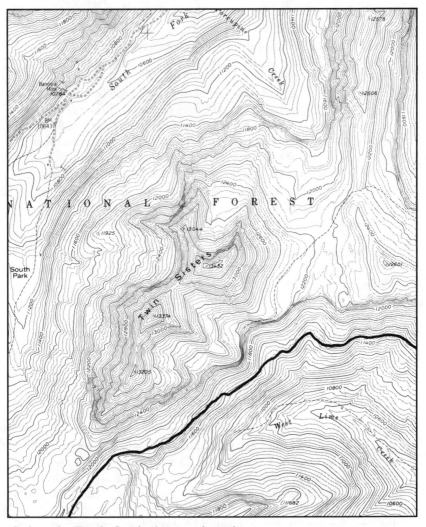

Colorado Trail, Sixth Access (west)

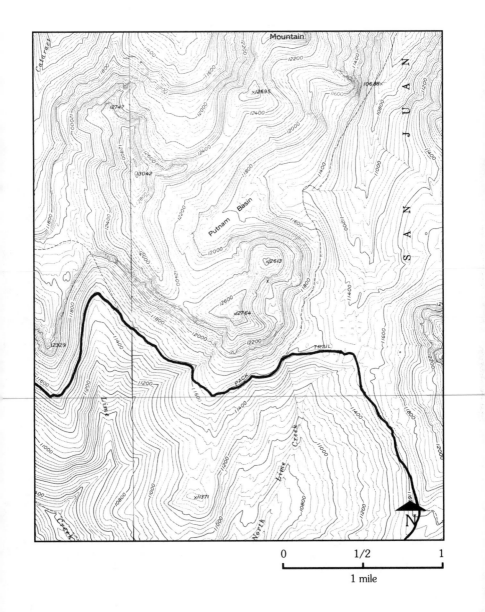

Mountain

SAN JUAN

Putnam   Basin

TRAIL

PACK

N

| 0 | | 1/2 | | 1 |

1 mile

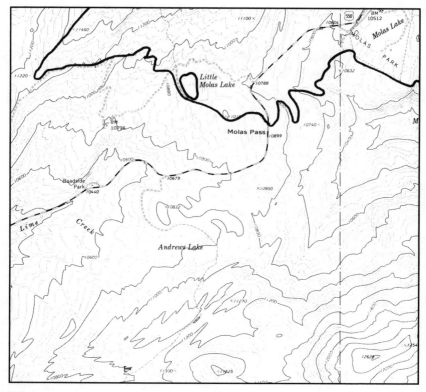

Colorado Trail, Sixth Access (east)

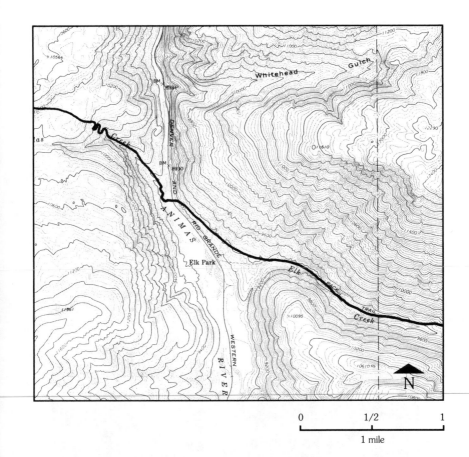

0   1/2   1

1 mile

The remains of a once-prosperous mill, with the ghost town of Tomboy in the distance behind, located at timberline between Ouray and Telluride.

Old boilers at the mill.

There is a third option for a starting point. Go on north on the highway beyond the Molas Trail turnoff to the next turnoff, which takes you into Molas Lake, a privately operated recreational spot. There is a store here where you can get any provisions for the hike you may need; there is also fishing and camping. With permission you can park here and start your hike south to the descending Molas Trail, then follow it on east to the river.

Appendix—Tread Lightly

Most of the hikes described in this book are on national forest land, some are on land administered by the U.S. Bureau of Land Management, a tiny bit is on private land. In any land use, responsible-usage ethics are essential. The forest service and Bureau of Land Management have cooperated in promoting such an ethic under the title "Tread Lightly." Most of the problems of land deterioration due to human traffic have arisen in connection with vehicles: four-wheel-drives, all-terrain vehicles (ATVs), mountain bicycles, dirt motorcycles, and snowmobiles. These are all great recreational vehicles that can be used for fun and profit in the backcountry, but they cause much damage to the land and general environment if proper precautions are not observed—so much so that damaged spots have to be closed to them at times. Hikers are much less trouble, but they can cause some damage, especially in high-use areas. Also, hikers often use some of these vehicles to get to trailheads; thus, they need to be aware of and observe good environmental ethics, too.

The pledge developed for this program follows:

I Pledge to TREAD LIGHTLY by:

Traveling only where motorized vehicles are permitted.

Respecting the rights of hikers, skiers, campers, and others to enjoy their activities undisturbed.

Educating myself by obtaining travel maps and regulations from public agencies, complying with signs and barriers, and asking owners' permission to cross private land.

Avoiding streams, lakeshores, meadows, muddy roads and trails, steep hillsides, wildlife, and livestock.

Driving responsibly to protect the environment and preserve opportunities to enjoy my vehicle on wild lands.

The pledge is for vehicle use. Hikers need to observe other responsible-use practices as well; for instance, carrying out all trash; avoiding walking in eroded areas; taking care not to damage tender, sensitive plants; and avoiding the disturbance of wildlife.

The forest service and Bureau of Land Management offices carry additional materials about this program. There are

A well-preserved tower for tram cables once used to carry ore across difficult terrain.

information brochures, bumper stickers, shoulder patches, and individual logos for each separate type of transportation in the backcountry including hiking and skiing.

The San Juan National Forest has an auxiliary volunteer support organization, the San Juan National Forest Association, which you may be interested in getting information from, or even joining. It states its purpose thus: "The SJNFA is a non-profit organization which helps the U.S. Forest Service promote public education, conservation, and interpretation of natural and cultural resources. Our goal is to instill in the public a land ethic . . . a sense of pride and stewardship toward our public lands." Among other things, the association currently publishes relevant books, pamphlets, video and audio tapes, and maps. They help in the forest with trails, campsites, and archeological projects, and they sponsor workshops, seminars, and research projects.

For further information, contact the San Juan National Forest Association, P.O. Box 2261, Durango, Colorado 81302; (970) 385-1210; fax (970) 385-1224.

Index